THE

QUEEN
VICTORIA

SERIES EDITOR: Bonnie G. Smith, Rutgers University

Published

ANWAR al-SADAT: *Transforming the Middle East*
Robert L. Tignor

MUSTAFA KEMAL ATATÜRK: *Heir to an Empire*
Ryan Gingeras

MARGARET THATCHER: *Shaping the New Conservatism*
Meredith Veldman

QUEEN VICTORIA: *Gender and Empire*
Susan Kingsley Kent

Forthcoming

MALIK AMBAR: *Power and Slavery Across the Indian Ocean*
Omar H. Ali

SIMONE DE BEAUVOIR: *Creating a Feminine Existence*
Sandrine Sanos

LIN ZEXU: *Imperial China in a Globalizing World*
David Atwill

THE WORLD IN A LIFE

THE LIVES OF PEOPLE and the unfolding of earth-shaking events inspire us to love history. We live in a global age where big concepts such as "globalization" often tempt us to forget the "people" side of the past. The titles in *The World in a Life* series aim to revive these meaningful lives. Each one shows us what it felt like to live on a world historical stage and even to shape the world's destiny.

The lives of most individuals are full of activity and color and even passion and violence. The people examined in *The World in a Life* series often faced outsized challenges, but they usually met the great events of their day energetically. They lived amidst enormous change, as we often do. Their lives show us how to navigate change and to find solutions. They made fateful decisions, often with much soul-searching or—as often—on the spur of the moment and even intuitively. We have much to learn from these fateful past lives.

Their actions, however, were filled with complexity. Biographies in this series give a "nutshell" explanation of how important paradoxes and dilemmas have been in the stories of individuals operating on the world stage. Their lives become windows onto the complicated trends, events, and crises of their time, providing an entry point for a deeper understanding of a particular historical era. As such events and crises unfolded, these historical figures also faced crises in their personal lives. In the intertwined dramas of the personal and political, of the individual and the global, we come to understand the complexities of acting on the world stage and living in world history.

BONNIE G. SMITH
Rutgers University

QUEEN VICTORIA

GENDER AND EMPIRE

SUSAN KINGSLEY KENT

New York Oxford
OXFORD UNIVERSITY PRESS

Oxford University Press is a department of the University of Oxford.
It furthers the University's objective of excellence in research,
scholarship, and education by publishing worldwide.

Oxford   New York
Auckland   Cape Town   Dar es Salaam   Hong Kong   Karachi
Kuala Lumpur   Madrid   Melbourne   Mexico City   Nairobi
New Delhi   Shanghai   Taipei   Toronto

With offices in
Argentina   Austria   Brazil   Chile   Czech Republic   France   Greece
Guatemala   Hungary   Italy   Japan   Poland   Portugal   Singapore
South Korea   Switzerland   Thailand   Turkey   Ukraine   Vietnam

Copyright © 2016 by Oxford University Press

Published by Oxford University Press
198 Madison Avenue, New York, New York 10016
http://www.oup.com

Oxford is a registered trademark of Oxford University Press.

Library of Congress Cataloging-in-Publication Data
Kent, Susan Kingsley, 1952 May 9-
    Queen Victoria : gender and empire / Susan Kingsley Kent,
University of Colorado, Boulder.
      pages cm. -- (The World in a Life)
    Includes index.
    ISBN 978-0-19-025000-3 (pbk. : alk. paper) 1. Victoria,
Queen of Great Britain, 1819-1901. 2. Queens -- Great Britain --
Biography. 3. Great Britain -- History -- Victoria, 1837-1901. I. Title.
    DA554.K46 2015
    941.081092--dc23
    [B]
                                                    2015008405

Printing number: 9 8 7 6 5 4 3 2 1

Printed in the United States of America
on acid-free paper

FOR MY MOTHER

CONTENTS

List of Illustrations   xi

List of Maps   xii

Acknowledgments   xiii

About the Author   xiv

Introduction   1

1. CHILDHOOD, 1819–1837: TRANSITION TO A NEW SOCIAL AND POLITICAL ORDER   3

2. QUEEN, WIFE, MOTHER: SEPARATE SPHERE IDEOLOGY AND THE PARADOX OF FEMALE MONARCHY, 1840–1861   36

3. CO-RULERS, 1842–1861: CHANGING IDEOLOGIES OF GENDER AND RACE   63

4. THE WIDOWED QUEEN, 1861–1872   93

5. REEMERGENCE, 1873–1887: NEW IMPERIALISM AND NEW CHALLENGES TO SEPARATE SPHERES   123

6.   THE HEIGHT OF VICTORIA'S REIGN, 1887–1901:
GENDER, JUBILEES, AND COLONIAL WARS   151

7.   THE LEGACY OF THE LATE QUEEN   175

Primary Source Excerpts and Study Questions   182
Further Reading   190
Notes   196
Credits   204
Index   205

LIST OF ILLUSTRATIONS

1. Victoria as a child with her mother,
   Victoria, Duchess of Kent   16

2. John Conroy   18

3. Queen Victoria's First Council, 1837   37

4. Queen Victoria and Lord Melbourne, 1838   38

5. Marriage of Queen Victoria and Prince
   Albert, 1840   45

6. Queen Victoria with Albert and their family, 1860   55

7. Victoria's goddaughter, Sarah Forbes Bonetta, 1862   73

8. Irish Potato Famine, 1846   75

9. Indian Mutiny, 1857   81

10. Queen Victoria and children in mourning, 1862   95

11. Queen Victoria with John Brown at Balmoral, 1863   97

12. Benjamin Disraeli buys Suez Canal shares, 1876   124

13. Queen Victoria proclaimed Empress of India
    in Delhi, 1877   127

14. Victoria decorating officers engaged in the Zulu
    Wars, 1879   130

15. Cartoon of Victoria and Cecil Rhodes   163

16. Women and children transported to camps during
    South African War, 1901   172

17. Funeral of Queen Victoria, 1901   173

LIST OF MAPS

1. The British Empire in 1837   23

2. Africa in 1870   132

3. Africa in 1900   133

4. The British Empire in 1900   168

ACKNOWLEDGMENTS

LIKE ITS SUBJECT following the death of her beloved husband, this short biography of Queen Victoria spent a number of years well out of public view. That it now sees the light of day is due solely to the commitment and perseverance of Bonnie Smith, Priscilla McGeehon, and Charles Cavaliere. I thank them for all the time, energy, and effort they put into conceiving and executing the project and for including me in *The World in a Life* series. I am proud to be in the company of its authors and editors.

I am indebted to Paul Hammer and Thea Lindquist, my colleagues at the University of Colorado, for their suggestions and assistance in gaining access to primary sources. Anonymous readers pointed out deficiencies and gave excellent advice, for which I am most grateful. Lynn Luecken at OUP managed the complicated process of bringing the series to completion with efficiency and good humor. Lori Bradshaw and Leslie Anglin ensured that my mistakes were kept to a minimum. Many thanks to you all.

ABOUT THE AUTHOR

SUSAN KINGSLEY KENT is professor of history at the University of Colorado, Boulder. Her publications include *Sex and Suffrage in Britain, 1860–1914* (1987); *Making Peace: The Reconstruction of Gender in Interwar Britain* (1993); *Gender and Power in Britain, 1640–1990* (1999); *Aftershocks: Politics and Trauma in Interwar Britain* (2010); *The Global Flu Pandemic of 1918–1919* (2012); *The Women's War of 1929: Gender and Violence in Colonial Nigeria* (2011), with Misty Bastian and Marc Matera; *Gender and History* (2011); and *Africans and Britons in the Age of Empires, 1660–1980* (2015), with Myles Osborne. In addition, Professor Kent is the author of an e-text with Great River Technologies entitled *The History of Western Civilization Since 1500: An Ecological Approach.*

INTRODUCTION

AS THE LONGEST REIGNING MONARCH in British history, Queen Victoria gave her name to an age filled with enormous possibilities and perplexing contradictions. Her life and rule exemplified some of those contradictions, and an examination of them through the lens of gender and empire enables us to see and appreciate how they played out.

At the time of Victoria's birth, Britain ruled over what was fast becoming the greatest empire in the world, containing millions of non-white, non-Christian peoples. During her childhood and youth, the kingdom itself became transformed from one dominated by landed aristocrats to one governed according to the principles of bourgeois liberalism. The royal family served as the most visible symbol of domesticity, while at the same time Victoria's very position as queen defied the ideology of separate spheres upon which domesticity rested. This would make for difficulties within her marriage to Albert in the early years, as he struggled to find his place in a man's world ruled by a woman, who in turn found herself in the middle of shifting understandings about the nature and role of monarchical power. Gender and power were tricky things that required careful negotiation.

In private, contrary to everything we think we know about Victoria and the prudery of the period, she and Albert shared an intimate relationship of robust vitality. Childbirth was another story, however, a travail to which Victoria never reconciled herself. She found great comfort in chloroform and in making public its effectiveness and respectability—at least through the medical profession—eased the confinements of millions of women.

1

Victoria, the ruler of millions of people, opposed women participating in politics or public life. She was appalled by the prospect of women becoming physicians, seeing them as indecent. She believed women's suffrage to be a "wicked folly" and a violation of God's laws. She never gave up that belief, even as the mid-century, fledging feminist movement matured and grew to the size of a mass movement. And yet she reigned, with little thought of the contradictions that entailed.

Victoria's participation in politics turns out to have been far more direct than we have been led to believe by theorists like Walter Bagehot. She was no mere figurehead, but intervened in some of the most important issues of the day. Many of those issues concerned the empire, where she acted decisively to alter the course of events. The failure to enact a home rule bill for Ireland and the split in the Liberal party that resulted is but one example of her refusal to sit on the sidelines.

Over the span of Victoria's reign, the size, composition, and character of the British Empire changed dramatically. From one purported to be based on liberal principles in the first half of the nineteenth century, it emerged after the Indian Mutiny of 1857 in far more belligerent and autocratic form and tone. Despite Victoria's love for "her" subjects, imperial rule became hard and aggressive. As Empress of India after 1877, she presided over "new imperial" projects across the globe as Europeans vied with one another to expand their power. The last fifteen years of Victoria's life saw an enormous expansion of empire, as the so-called scramble for Africa took place.

At home, feminist campaigns to enable women to own property, to gain entry into professions, and to end what amounted to the legalization of prostitution won important and lasting victories. The ultimate goal—votes for women on the same lines as they were granted to men—remained unmet by the time the great queen died, but it would not be long before even that end was finally attained.

CHAPTER 1

| CHILDHOOD, 1819–1837: |
TRANSITION TO A NEW SOCIAL
AND POLITICAL ORDER

ALEXANDRINA VICTORIA KENT, the infant who would become
Queen Victoria, entered the world on May 24, 1819. The only
child of Prince Edward, the Duke of Kent, and Victoria, Princess
Regent of the small German state of Leiningen, Victoria hailed
from families with long royal pedigrees. Her father was the fourth
son of Britain's King George III; her mother, the sister of the
Duke of Saxe-Coburg and of the man who would become
Leopold I, King of the Belgians. Ordinarily, a child of a royal son
positioned so far down the line of succession would not expect to
ascend to the British throne, but the situation had dramatically
changed in 1817, when Princess Charlotte, the daughter of
George, the heir to the throne, and Princess Caroline, died giving
birth to a stillborn son. Charlotte's father would become George
IV in 1820, but with no heir, the line of succession moved to
George's seven brothers and their progeny. Only four of the
brothers proved eligible to produce a royal heir, the others having
married or taken common-law wives outside of the bounds of
legitimacy as it had been defined in the Royal Marriages Act of
1772. The Duke of Kent emerged as the most promising figure to

carry on the royal line, and Victoria's birth signaled the appearance of a potential future queen.

Victoria's importance to the continuation of the Hanoverian line of the British monarchy increased within months of her birth. Her father, fourth in line to inherit the throne, died on January 23, 1820, when Victoria was only eight months old. Her grandfather, the mad King George III, died six days later. And the new king, George IV, became seriously ill shortly thereafter, raising the prospect of two dead kings in the space of a month. George IV did not die, as it turned out, but the scare made it abundantly clear that the infant Victoria held a position of great significance.

Victoria's birth occurred at a time when the political, economic, social, and domestic regimes of Britain were undergoing profound alteration in some crucial aspects of which she and her family would play a significant role in later years. The process of transitioning from an aristocratic to a bourgeois liberal system had begun in the late eighteenth century, when aristocratic norms of behavior and forms of domestic arrangements came under fire from a variety of groups, and a series of behaviors identified with the middle classes began to hold greater sway in society. Informed by the precepts of evangelical Christianity and political economy and inspired by the disorders produced by industrialization and the French Revolution, a small but influential group of male and female reformers organized in the so-called Clapham sect set about the dual tasks of bringing spiritual renewal and social order to a nation that had, as they saw it, fallen into moral degeneracy. Under the leadership of Hannah More, the evangelical campaign to strengthen the social hierarchy and reform the "manners and morals" of the nation proceeded apace, attracting widespread support from men, and particularly women, of the mercantile and landed middling classes.

Moral regeneration, in the eyes of evangelicals, could be achieved only through individual faith in the grace of God, and the best place for such faith to be sustained, they held, was in the home. Social improvement and a renewed respect for social hierarchy, it followed, required Britons to practice self-discipline in all aspects of their lives, whether refraining from alcohol consumption, gambling, or sexual activity. These were qualities that the poor would have to be taught, and it devolved upon women of the middling ranks, as guardians of the domestic sphere and of morality, to serve as their instructors. Calling upon middling women to "come forward with a patriotism at once firm and feminine for the general good," Hannah More urged them in 1799 to "contribute their full and fair proportion toward the saving of their country," to "raise the depressed tone of public morals, to awaken the drowsy spirit of religious principle, and to re-animate the dormant powers of active piety." But they were to do so, she insisted, in accordance with her position on women appearing in public, "without departing from the refinement of their character, without derogating from the dignity of their rank; without blemishing the delicacy of their sex." Social stability demanded that middling women eschew any claim to political or legal rights, that they sacrifice their personal aspirations to public activity or equality with men to the higher religious and social goals of deference, hierarchy, and authority. They must learn, and pass on to their working-class charges, habits of restraint. "They should, when very young, be inured to contradiction," More advised. "They should be led to distrust their own judgment; they should learn not to murmur at expostulation; but should be accustomed to expect and endure opposition.... It is of the last importance to their happiness in life that they should early acquire a submissive temper and a forbearing spirit."[1]

Disciplining themselves and others in the ways of submissiveness, self-denial, and dependence, More assured the readers of her wildly successful *Cheap Repository of Moral and Religious Tracts*,[2] of which several million were printed, sold, and/or disseminated among the plebeian classes around the turn of the century, would advance the cause of domestic purity and moral regeneration of society. The family, in the *Cheap Repository Tracts*, offered shelter from a world of sin and temptation: within the home, men received the care and attention of diligent, indus-trious, sober, pious, and honest wives; children learned the lessons that would guide them throughout the rest of their life at the feet of their parents. These virtues promised all of them a peaceable, happy, harmonious, and comfortable existence.

But beyond that, these were the qualities and values neces-sary to uphold the new industrial order of factories and disci-plined workforces. One of the first lessons middling women would have to impart if morality and civility were to be attained by the working classes, More asserted, was the folly and the danger of women going out to work. They would have to be taught domestic "oeconomy," the art of keeping a home neat, orderly, and provisioned on a very small income. In the minds of evangel-icals and political economists, an arrangement of separate spheres for men and women, in which men went out to work while their wives remained at home to maintain a decent, moral, disciplined, and well-regulated domestic life, provided the building blocks upon which a stable, hierarchical, deferential social order could be constructed and sustained in the midst of industrial transfor-mation and political revolution.

The proponents of evangelicalism and of political economy, many of them, like Hannah More, one and the same person, helped to establish among the middling and elite ranks, if not yet among the working classes and the poor, models of masculinity and femininity that prevailed throughout the nineteenth cen-tury. Even among aristocratic men, a new seriousness and moral earnestness began to take hold, superseding earlier aristocratic disdain for work, for instance, and replacing styles that emulated the "effeminate" French with those of a much more "manly," British, sometimes even military, cast. Wigs, powdered hair, the wearing of brightly colored silks, brocades, and laces—these gave way to a more understated, sober form of dress for upper-class men, characterized by breeches, boots, and a riding coat for rural elites, and dark-colored suits for those gentlemen who worked in London or other large towns. Their behavior, or at least prescriptions for it, underwent change as well, as notions of hard work, self-restraint, duty, religiosity, and faithfulness to marriage vows trickled upward into elite households. By 1800 it was no longer possible for politicians holding office to flaunt their keeping of mistresses, as it had been in the earlier part of the eighteenth century. Rather, they had to keep up the appearance, at least, of dedicated family men with a keen appreciation for their domestic responsibilities. By 1815, Britain's ruling elites, whose fitness to rule had been called into question throughout the eighteenth century by claims about their effeminacy, most recently by Thomas Paine's description of them as a "seraglio of males," had established themselves as the manly embodiments of discipline and authority. Elite women, for their part, espoused, even if they did not conform to, principles of domesticity that rendered women dependent, submissive, and passive, the guardians of morality and civility in a rapidly changing and increasingly dangerous world. The idea of upright, manly, respectable males operating in the public sphere of work and politics, supported and sustained in their endeavors by dependent, submissive, pure women operating in the domestic sphere of home and family, where their authority over all matters pertaining to morality and civility went uncontested—this ideological formulation of domesticity and separate spheres consolidated itself by the first decades of the nineteenth century and would serve as the paradigm for normative gender relations until the first decades of the twentieth.

Demands for moral regeneration accelerated in the period immediately following the defeat of Napoleon at Waterloo in 1815, years that saw much social distress as efforts to return to a peacetime economy produced severe dislocation, depression, and unemployment. Workers in virtually every sector of the economy suffered hardship, and it is likely that the real earnings of average working-class families in the years 1815 to 1819 fell below what they had been in the 1780s. Poor rates, which householders earning a certain income paid to alleviate destitution among the working poor, reached very high levels, an indication that more families than usual were unable to sustain themselves economically. In 1815, too, parliament passed the Corn Bill, which restricted the importation of wheat from outside Britain unless the price of domestic grain rose above a level that ensured farmers a handsome profit. The Corn Law benefitted landowners by limiting competition from abroad, but it hurt working people by making the price of bread more dear. Riots protesting the high cost of bread broke out across England in the fall of 1815, followed by a rash of machine breaking by so-called Luddites in many of the industrial areas in 1816.

The dismal economic conditions of postwar life contributed to the propensity of many working-class men and women to join with middle-class activists in demanding parliamentary reform. The Corn Law, in particular, symbolized for reformers the abuses of a parliamentary system made up of privileged, self-interested, landowning elites—aristocrats and gentry. The reform movement, a disparate group made up of Whigs sitting in parliament, of middling people outside of parliament seeking far-reaching reform along constitutional lines, and a number of popular radicals willing to engage in extralegal and even violent means to bring about significant political changes, sought to eliminate the "old corruption" of aristocratic government and to replace it with annual parliaments elected on the basis of a wider suffrage. Only in this way, reformers believed, could cronyism, favoritism, corruption, and the influence of the House of Lords and the Anglican Church be stamped out and good government designed to further the interests of the people as a whole be implemented.

Radicals often framed their attack on aristocracy and old corruption in languages of gender and sexuality. In the early nineteenth century, "dandies" like the Prince of Wales, one of Victoria's "wicked uncles," and his hangers-on at court received the brunt of radical criticism. Because they paid careful attention to their appearance, wore extravagant clothing, and flaunted a lifestyle that eschewed work of any sort, they could easily be rendered "feminine" by their detractors. The radical paper,

The Black Dwarf, for instance, attacked aristocratic manhood in 1818 by describing elites as "a new race of men" who "wear stays, and drink God to save the King, in dandy punch. Their gender is not yet ascertained," it proclaimed, "but as their principal ambition seems to be to look as pretty as women, it would be most uncharitable to call them men." One semipornographic squib had the Prince Regent proclaiming, as he indulged his various appetites, "For the good of the people this carcase so brawny/I fatten with Turtle and mullogatawney./For the good of the people I spend on a—[whore]/What else would be wasted on ten thousand poor." These attacks on aristocratic effeminacy sought to undermine the legitimacy of elite rule and to buttress the case for radical reform by associating it with manliness. As one working man put it at a December 1816 reform meeting in Middleton, "it was impossible for a Reform to take place whilst the Leaders of the Constitution were going on in wantonness and lust."[3]

What became known as the Queen Caroline affair provided radicals and reformers with an opportunity to demonstrate their defense of and claim to virtue in opposition to what they regarded as aristocratic tyranny and oppression. In 1820, the year following Victoria's birth, George IV became king after many years of ruling as Prince Regent on behalf of his incapacitated father, George III. His estranged and ill-treated wife, Caroline, who had been in self-imposed exile in Europe since 1814, when she agreed to leave England in return for an annual payment of £35,000, returned, demanding that she be recognized as queen. George responded with an action for divorce in the House of Lords, causing a Bill of Pains and Penalties to be brought against her that censured her for adultery and rescinded her queenly status. Coming from a man whom the radical press had denounced as a lecherous dandy, whose regency had been characterized by profligacy and debauchery, making it an irresistible magnet for charges of financial and political as well as moral corruption, the new king's charges met with an outburst of popular fury against what was perceived as the latest, most egregious, manifestation of "old corruption." In the melodrama that followed, Caroline, whose behavior while in Europe was hardly pristine, took on the trappings of the "poor wronged female," a poor forlorn woman, whose virtue, sullied by an evil king and his equally evil ministers, must be defended by the manly, courageous people of Britain.

The radical press exploited the scandal with ferocious and obscene satire, taking every opportunity to draw connections between old corruption and the campaign against Caroline. Pamphleteers published accounts of adulterous liaisons on the part of the king's men who had brought action against the queen and noted the salaries and pensions of those in the House of Lords who opposed her as a means of bringing to light the sordid workings of unreformed government. William Benbow, a radical publisher, ran a print charging that the state's evidence against Caroline had been produced by bribing spies from Italy to lie about her behavior there, bribes financed with money stolen from hardworking, honest English soldiers and sailors who had only five years before given their all to protect their country against foreign aggression. In *Fair Play, or Who Are the Adulterers, Slanderers and Demoralizers?*, Benbow insisted that "there is not a jury in the United Kingdom, would believe the filthy testimony of the filthy witnesses, arranged by the filthy junta, employed for the base, unmanly and iniquitous purpose of dethroning a Queen."[4]

The Queen Caroline affair, by linking the somewhat abstract constitutional concerns of radicalism—the role of the monarch in government, corruption and patronage, and the infringement by parliament on the liberties of the people—with the immediately personal and moral concerns of people in their everyday lives, gave radicalism a base of popular support that it had not enjoyed since the days of the civil war of the mid-seventeenth century. "The people all favour the Queen," noted Lady Palmerston, "including the respectable middle ranks." Anti-king feeling ran high, and the king's ministers feared for the survival of the throne. William Lamb, who would become Lord Melbourne, the queen's indispensable advisor, wrote to William Wilberforce "that there appears to be a great danger of serious popular tumult and insurrection."[5]

For men, the misuse of Caroline by George and his ministers resonated with the grievances plebeians and radicals experienced at the hands of "aristocratic government." Referring to the economic distress of the postwar years, the Artisans, Mechanics, and Labouring Classes of Manchester in September 1820 commiserated with the Queen. "The same power which scourged us, is now oppressing you," they declared. In Nottingham, the *Black Dwarf* reported, the people "felt for the wrongs of the Queen as they felt for the various oppressions under which they themselves labored." By mixing the personal with the constitutional, the private with the public, working people were better able to internalize the more distant concerns of political reform and make them their own. As long-time radical Major John Cartwright observed, "the honor of the Queen is closely related with the constitutional rights of the people." Caroline exploited this sentiment regularly, telling an audience in London that "those who degrade the Queen have never manifested any repugnance in abridging the liberties of the people." "My loss of rank," she explained at another time, "would have been their loss of liberties."[6]

Women of the plebeian and middling ranks rallied massively on behalf of Caroline. Addresses bearing the signatures of tens of thousands of women from across Britain proclaimed their support for the queen, and gave expression to the fear that if the action against Caroline succeeded then they, the virtuous women of Britain, could find no security against men in their own lives. Caroline told an audience of women that "if my matrimonial rights are illegally annulled, theirs eventually may be rendered less secure." A number of Ladies of Edinburgh, agreed, proclaiming in an address:

> The principles and doctrines now advanced by your accusers, do not apply to your case alone, but if made part of the law of the

land may hereafter be applied as a precedent from every careless
and dissipated husband to rid himself of his wife, however good
and innocent she may be; and to render his family, however amiable, illegitimate, thereby destroying the sacred bond of matrimony, and rendering all domestic felicity very uncertain.

As one widely heard ballad phrased women's concerns,
"Attend ye virtuous British wives/Support your injured Queen,/
Assert her rights; they are your own,/As plainly may be seen."[7]

The rights of women referred to in this ballad were not political ones. Instead, they denoted the right to respect, safety, and
security that women, because of their sex, deserved from men.
The *Black Dwarf* reminded its readers that "no man would basely
forfeit the love and esteem of his wife, his daughters, his sisters, or
his mistress, by calmly suffering the violation of every female
right in the person of his Queen." Radical William Hone exhorted working men to come to the aid of the queen on the
grounds that "the beauty—the goodness—the very helplessness
of the sex are so many . . . sacred calls on the assistance of every
manly and courageous arm." In urging plebeian men "To assert
the Rights of Man/To avenge the Wrongs of Woman," radical
leaders were not merely insisting on the relationship of politics to
virtue; they were incorporating upper- and middle-class evangelical ideals of separate sphere ideology into their radical rhetoric
and directing them at working men and women. In the process,
they helped to occasion a significant shift in the ways radical
working-class men defined and understood their masculinity. In
defending the virtue of the wronged queen, plebeian men took on
the chivalric role of protector of all women, an image that countered the picture of plebeians as libertine and immoral in the
countless *Cheap Repository Tracts* put out by evangelicals.[8]

Plebeian women did not necessarily accept the prescription
of separate spheres without some revision of its terms. Calling
upon their own experiences and upon earlier working-class traditions of female industriousness, courage, and competency, many

working-class women celebrated Caroline as a fearless, reasonable, educated heroine, ascribing to her qualities that went far beyond those of helplessness, passivity, and sexual purity. Benbow's "Glorious Deeds of Women" placed Caroline in a pantheon of heroines that included Joan of Arc and Charlotte Corday. Anne Cobbett, daughter of radical leader William Cobbett, painted a portrait of the queen that combined the traits of the now-conventional upper- and middle-class woman of domesticity with those of a larger womanhood. She is "a real *good woman*, kind, charitable, feeling and condescending toward every creature." At the same time, wrote Cobbett, "she possesses wonderful courage, presence of mind, fortitude, promptness in action. . . . She is very industrious."[9]

Despite the wider scope given to Caroline by working-class women's depictions of her, it was her traditional status as wife and mother that enabled her to serve as a rallying point for such diverse constituencies. Middle-class women saw in her a virtuous female in need of male protection. Support for Caroline constituted support for the institution of marriage and a rejection of divorce; it shored up the boundaries of separate spheres. Plebeian women identified with her mistreatment at the hands of her husband and applauded her courage in resisting him. To middle-class men, she offered an opportunity for them to assert their morality against the libertinism of the aristocracy, thus buttressing their claims for political reform by playing on the age-old concepts of virtue against corruption. For working-class men, she represented their own political grievances against oppression and tyranny and enabled them to demonstrate their respectability as manly defenders of innocent, downtrodden females.

As it turned out, the political agenda of radicalism became subsumed under the personal, moral, and domestic concerns raised by the Queen Caroline affair. The House of Lords did indeed pass a Bill of Pains and Penalties against Caroline in October 1820, but by so narrow a margin that the government withdrew it, acknowledging its defeat at the hands of the people.

But the victory of the people in this sordid episode did not translate into governmental reform. Instead, radicalism as a political force rapidly lost its vigor and its numbers, as middle-class reformers and Whigs in parliament abandoned their alliance with the popular classes and as improving economic conditions after 1820 weakened the appeal of radical politics for masses of working people. Radicalism did not disappear, but just as its popularity had skyrocketed during the Queen Caroline affair, so too it plummeted back to earth with her acquittal and with her acceptance from the government in January 1821 of an annual pension of £50,000.

Although the political radicalism of the affair faded away, at least for the short term, the scandal nonetheless had a lasting impact on and consequences for all ranks of society. The events of the first year of Princess Victoria's life marked a historical moment when one societal model of marriage and sexuality was decisively thrown over for another. The evangelical domestic ideal, with its concomitant emphases on separate spheres for men and women; the sanctity of marriage and family; passivity, morality, and purity for women; and sobriety and respectability for men, gained a hold over British life that prevailed for the rest of the century. At the very top, it would no longer be possible for royals, and by extension, aristocrats, to behave publicly in a debauched, libertine, profligate manner. Britons had made it clear that their king, if he was to be the father of the people, would be a husband to his wife as well; a true husband of devotion, fidelity, and morality. As the "Ode to George the Fourth and Caroline his wife," implored the king, "A *Father* to the *nation* prove,/A *Husband* to thy *Queen*,/And safely in thy people's Love,/Reign tranquil and serene."[10]

In the persons of King William, who followed George IV upon his death in 1830, and his consort Adelaide, Britain obtained a royal family that seemed to exude domesticity, even if William's ten children by his first, common-law wife gave the lie to royal morals. Victoria's accession to the throne in 1837 completed the domestication of the monarchy, a story we will take up in Chapter 2. Ironically, the Queen Caroline affair, which had threatened to bring down the monarchy in 1820, served instead to strengthen it in the eyes of the British people.

Upper- and middle-class women, if not yet working-class women, received overwhelming public affirmation of a way of life—domesticity and separate spheres—that promised them protection, respect, security, and an arena in which they could play an influential role. The country's domestic virtue—the defense of the private sphere of home and family, and, most important, the care of and solicitation paid to the women who inhabited it—supporters of Caroline claimed insistently, marked Britain as a civilization superior to all others. The treatment of women at the hands of men became a prime measure of civility in British eyes, and would be used to evaluate the credibility of claims to citizenship by middle- and working-class men and for self-government on the part of colonized peoples. The elevation of women's status to a criterion of national greatness, and of women to the position of "the angel in the house," did not meet the approval of everyone, as we shall see later, but it did reflect a societal transformation in attitudes about women that could have positive results. No longer the embodiments of evil and carnality, as they had been construed in the eighteenth century, upper- and middle-class women, at least, commanded the respect and concern of the nation.

For middle-class men, the attack on Caroline by her husband and his ministers served to point up in no uncertain terms the corrupt nature and injustice of aristocratic rule, undermining its authority considerably. Moreover, it enabled them to claim an active role for themselves in a reformed system of government on the grounds of their superior virtue, of the manliness of their men in defending the purity and honor of Caroline, and by extension, of their own wives and daughters. In possessing virtue, now defined as the keeping of chaste, modest women in the private sphere of the home and family, middle-class men asserted their respectability, their fitness for participating in the politics of the nation.

Victoria as a child with her mother, Victoria, Duchess of Kent.

Upon the death of her father, Victoria came largely under the sway of her mother's German relations and contacts. Still a distant figure in the line of succession to the throne, the young princess commanded little attention from George IV; he regarded Victoria's mother, the Duchess of Kent, with suspicion and disdain and refused to settle upon her the kind of resources Victoria believed she needed to establish a proper household. But more than Hanoverian antipathy to the Kents brought about this isolation from the court. Given the contempt with which much of the country regarded the king and his household, the duchess felt it crucial for Victoria's ultimate success to dissociate the princess from any connection with them. For Victoria's succession to the

throne was far from a fait accompli—not only did her wicked
uncles hold prior claims to hers, but some of them, like the Duke
of Cumberland, would contest Victoria's right even after parliament had designated her heir presumptive in 1830. The Duchess
of Kent had both to cement Victoria's place in the line of succession *and* in the hearts of the British people. This latter strategy
required that the princess be—and be shown to be—a model of
the kind of morality and rectitude that a significant portion of the
country had begun to expect of their rulers. The courts of George
IV and of his successor, William IV (who resided at Windsor
Castle with his ten children by his common-law wife prior to
his marriage to the woman who would become his queen consort), were hardly the places where these kinds of qualities
would shine. As the Duchess of Kent wrote to the Duchess of
Northumberland:

> Victoria is not to be fashionable, but is to acquire that equality of
> *dignity* that will affect all clases [sic]: I wish my child to be a pattern
> of female decorum—as to example—and *associates*—that every
> one may be sure of her *even* course. . . . I never did, neither will I
> now, associate Victoria in any way with the illegitimate [sic] mem-
> bers of the Royal family:—With the King they die; did I not keep
> this line how would it be possible to teach Victoria the difference
> betwen [sic] Vice and Virtue.[11]

Victoria saw her Hanoverian uncles, including Kings George
and William, only rarely. Instead, her upbringing lay in the hands
of her mother; her mother's brother, Leopold, who, until he
became King of Belgium in 1831, lived in England; and her mother's advisor, Sir John Conroy, a man whose ambition for power
and status was surpassed only by his delusions of grandeur. After
Leopold's departure for Belgium, the duchess and Conroy determined Victoria's actions and education exclusively, ushering in a
regime known as the Kensington system, so-called because the
family resided in Kensington Palace. By it, the young princess

would be isolated from virtually all outside influences and inculcated in the qualities best suited to a future queen. Conroy and the Duchess of Kent intended to control that young queen to their own ends, and they embarked on a campaign of disparagement, belittlement, and emotional abuse of the princess to ensure that outcome. Although they were ultimately thwarted in their efforts when Victoria became queen in her own right, having achieved maturity at the age of eighteen just months before the death of William IV, their suffocating efforts made Victoria's childhood and youth a lonely and difficult time for her. Her companions were chosen for her, often from among Conroy's children, whom she despised, and she was never permitted to be

John Conroy.

alone: She was required to sleep in her mother's bedroom every night and was not allowed to walk downstairs without someone holding her hand.

A good part of Victoria's education consisted of imparting the principles of proper womanhood laid out by Hannah More and other evangelical writers. In fact, More had written a tract explicitly addressed to Princess Charlotte in 1805 entitled *Hints Towards Forming the Character of a Young Princess*, in which she delineated what virtues and skills should be inculcated in the presumptive future queen of Great Britain. Because she advised a future ruler, More's curricular recommendations went beyond those one should expect for nonroyal girls—foreign language acquisition, in particular, would serve the princess well. But above all, the princess should be trained in the womanly virtues of meekness, patience, and obedience. The Duchess of Kent owned the fifth edition of More's *Hints*, published in 1819, which she likely used as the template for the education of her daughter Victoria. The duchess and Lord John Conroy had a clear stake in raising a potential future queen who would defer to them in all things; More's *Hints*, which the duchess gave to Victoria in 1835, a year in which the princess displayed a considerable amount of resistance to her keepers' efforts to control her, provided just the recipe for such an education.

Fortunately for Victoria, she possessed in her governess, Louise Lehzen (who would later be made a baroness), a secret ally in her struggle against the designs of her mother and the loathsome Conroy. Where they desired a subservient princess, Lehzen, as Victoria called her, sought to create a strong, intelligent, self-possessed woman. To that end, she and Victoria's tutor, the Reverend George Davys, established a curriculum for the princess that included history, law, geography, English composition, French, Latin, arithmetic, and religion. When in 1831, the Archbishop of Canterbury examined the eleven-year-old princess, he found her to have demonstrated "great intelligence."[12] Perhaps more important, Lehzen had encouraged in Victoria a fierce independence, self-discipline, and strength of character that would prove crucial to the ability of the young princess to determine her own fate. In 1835, while Victoria lay ill with what may have been typhoid fever, Conroy and her mother tried to force her to sign a document that would have made Conroy her personal secretary upon her accession as queen. Bedridden, weak, and feverish, Victoria, with Lehzen's invariable support, nevertheless withstood their imprecations. A year later, when her uncle Leopold tried to neutralize the influence of Conroy and the Duchess of Kent by foisting a husband of his choosing—his nephew, Albert—upon her, Victoria, again with Lehzen's support, demurred. She would ultimately marry Albert, but she did so on her terms as a queen in her own right, and not on anyone else's.

Between 1815 and 1832, middle- and working-class radicals joined together to push reform of the old regime, a union that broke apart when parliament offered middle-class men the vote, splitting them off from their erstwhile working-class and female allies. The Reform Act of 1832 signaled the triumph of liberalism over a far-reaching, more democratic radicalism. After 1832, a classical liberal political system derived from a franchise restricted by property qualifications and informed by the principles of meritocracy, individualism, free trade, and respectability supplanted the earlier regime comprised of patronage, deferential social relations, moral economy, and old corruption. Apologists for the middle classes, who gained political power with the Reform Act of 1832, explained their victory after the fact by referring to the so-called inherent bourgeois virtues of domesticity, drawing distinctions between the virtuous middle classes on the one hand, and the purportedly debauched aristocracy and equally immoral working classes on the other.

By the Reform Act of 1832, the radical vision of universal manhood suffrage and even of household suffrage was supplanted by a narrower view of political reform and citizenship that historians call classical liberalism. In its political guise, classical liberalism conferred citizenship and participation in government upon independent property owners. But under the law of coverture, married women had no rights or existence apart from their husbands. The popular aphorism "my wife and I are one and I am he" described a situation in which a married woman had no legal rights to her property, her earnings, her freedom of movement, her conscience, her body, or her children; all resided in her husband. Because married women could not own property under common law, and because unmarried women were considered the dependents of men within the family, citizenship, in liberal formulations, was denied them, as it was those men who did not own property or were dependent upon others, such as servants, laborers, or lodgers. For instance, James Mill's widely read "Article on Government," written in 1820, asserted that democratic political rights were necessitated by the laws of human nature that stated that "the ruling one or the ruling few, would, if checks did not operate in the way of prevention, reduce the great mass of the people subject to their power, at least to the condition of negroes in the West Indies." Having stated the Utilitarian case that only the widest political participation could ensure "the greatest happiness of the greatest number," Mill went on to qualify his claim. "One thing is pretty clear, that all those individuals whose interests are indisputably included in those of other individuals, may be struck off" the roster of political rights "without inconvenience." Among these he included "children up to a certain age" and women, "the interest of almost all of whom is involved either in that of their fathers or in that of their husbands." Working-class men, he asserted, could count on being looked after by "the most wise and virtuous part of the community, the middle rank."[13]

Indeed, the Reform Act of 1832 explicitly barred women from the franchise by using the phrase *every Male Person* to define those eligible to vote (though the Reform Act for Scotland in that same year delineated merely *every Person*) and by limiting it in the boroughs to those men who occupied premises that had an annual worth of £10, effectively ensuring that the newly enfranchised voters were of the respectable middle classes. Working men in a number of cities lost the right to vote in 1832, though over time, as inflation rendered the £10 criterion easier to meet, the numbers of working-class voters increased. Prior to 1832, perhaps one man in thirty enjoyed the right to vote; after 1832 that number rose to one in seven. Middle-class men, "the possessors of the wealth and intelligence of the country, the natural leaders of the physical force of the community," as MP Charles Buller described them, men whose commercial, financial, and industrial wealth could no longer be ignored by the ruling elites of Britain, were co-opted onto the side of order and conservatism to defeat working-class radical claims. Whig MP Thomas Babington Macaulay declared in the debate over the Reform Bill in 1831 that the middle classes offered a moderate middle ground between two extreme parties vying for control of government: "a narrow oligarchy above; an infuriated multitude below; on the one side the vices engendered by power; on the other side the vices engendered by distress." The middle classes, whose intelligence, hard work, steadiness, and respect for property inspired confidence that reform of political abuses rather than destruction of all property would follow their enfranchisement, Macaulay claimed, could be counted upon to prevent a collision between the two "vicious" extremes and "to save both from the fatal effects of their own folly."[14]

When the reformed parliament next met, it became clear to working-class radicals that their economic and familial concerns would not be redressed by a governing body informed by what were now deemed "middle-class" values. Instead, in keeping with those aspects of liberalism identified with political economy, parliament refused to entertain measures designed to alleviate conditions of work in factories and passed legislation creating a harsh, mean-spirited, and denigrating system of poor relief. For in addition to establishing principles of political rights and political liberties, classical liberalism stressed the rights of the individual to possess things. This cast on individual liberty gave activities

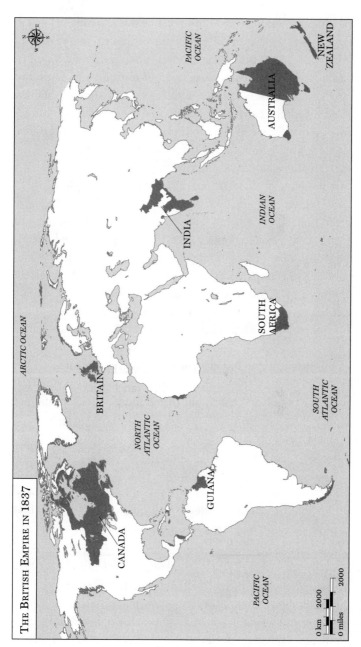

MAP 1. THE BRITISH EMPIRE IN 1837

relating to commerce and industry, like the amassing of capital, the rational utilization of labor and resources, the pursuit of self-improvement through education and training, and the cultivation of personal temperance and self-restraint a good deal of emphasis. Government's role, in the view of classical liberals, was to eliminate the barriers that hampered the exercise of these activities, to reform itself and to do away with practices, customs, laws, traditions, and ways of thinking that got in the way of the individual's right to have and benefit from his property, whether that property be material, moral, intellectual, or indeed, wives and children. Commercial and financial people, intellectuals, professionals, manufacturers, but also landed gentry seeking to improve their holdings and increase their wealth, found liberalism compatible with their interests and their outlooks. Evangelicals such as Hannah More and abolitionist William Wilberforce approved of liberalism's emphases on individual responsibility, self-improvement, morality, and self-restraint.

The throne Victoria would inherit in 1837 incorporated lands far beyond England, and it had done so for some time. The eighteenth-century British Empire generally conjures up an image of Britain's colonization of territories in North America, the West Indies, and India. But that empire is "British" and not merely "English" because England, over the space of two-and-a-half centuries, conquered and incorporated into the United Kingdom of Great Britain the countries of Wales, Scotland, and Ireland. Each country had come into the United Kingdom at different times, in different circumstances, and each experienced differential benefits from union with England. Over time, first the Welsh, who came into the United Kingdom of England and Wales in the early sixteenth century during the reign of Henry VIII, then the Scots after 1707, and finally, after 1801, the Protestants of Ireland, came to identify themselves and to be identified with Britain.

The Catholic Irish, on the other hand, who made up the vast majority of the population in Ireland, never ceased to consider themselves a colonized people whose fortunes were governed by a cruel imperial master of alien culture and religion. English overlordship of Ireland was buttressed by the plantation of thousands of English and Scottish settlers throughout the first two-thirds of the seventeenth century. When in 1688 James II fled to Ireland in advance of the armies of William of Orange, fought against him with the support of many Catholics, and lost, William and Mary exacted harsh revenge from Irish Catholics. Their penal code banished the Catholic clergy from Ireland; forbade Catholics to vote or to sit in parliament; banned them from teaching; from buying land, from leasing it for more than thirty-one years, from inheriting it from a Protestant, or from owning a horse worth more than £5; and excluded Irish shipping from the colonies, prohibited Irish woolen and glass exports from Britain, and made it unlawful to levy tariffs against English goods coming into Ireland. In virtually all respects, Irish subjection to England was complete.

From the time of the Tudors onward, the English justified their depredations against the Irish by portraying them as barbarous, primitive, pagan people whose country it was the responsibility of the English to inhabit and reform. One commentator described Irish society as a collection of people living like "beastes, void of lawe and all good order"; they were, he asserted, "more uncivill, more uncleanly, more barbarous and more brutish in their customs and demeanures, then [sic] in any other part of the world that is known." Just as the Romans had once brought civilization to a backward, uncivil, and uncouth England, declared Sir Thomas Smith, so too would the English persuade the Irish to engage "in vertuous labour and in justice, and . . . teach them our English lawes and civilitie and leave robbyng and stealing and killyng one of another."[15]

Depicting the Irish as by turns savage yet subtle, warlike but lazy, proud and cowardly, primitive yet cunning, English conquerors and observers of Ireland demonstrated a complicated mixture of attraction to and repulsion by Irish people and their mores. The Irish were dirty, violent, dishonest, lazy people who lived under inequitable and unjust laws, the English claimed, but they had nonetheless seduced and degenerated many an Englishman with their corrupt customs. The "wild shamrock manners"[16] of women, in particular, both shocked and titillated English travel writers, who saw in their refusal to wear corsets an intentional assertion of sexual invitation. Because Irish women partook of strong drink, presided over public feasts, and greeted strangers with a kiss; because their marriage laws permitted them to retain their names upon marriage and to divorce their husbands with relative ease and material support; because Irish custom permitted sexual relations within degrees of kin affinity far closer than those constituted by either English law or the Catholic clergy, English writers concluded that the women of Ireland held positions of authority over men at home and in public. Unmanly men and aggressive, sensualized, licentious women, they insisted, characterized social relations in Ireland, undermining good order and necessitating English intervention if civilization were ever to be established there. English observations of Irish culture and society contained frequent mention of exotic sexual activities and unconventional gender arrangements; languages of sexuality and gender, in other words, served to legitimate English conquest of foreign peoples. Long before Britain acquired an empire of people of different races, religions, and cultures in Africa and Asia in the late eighteenth and nineteenth centuries, Ireland served as a model of subject peoples in need of British civilization. The Irish, wrote Phillip Luckombe in 1783, "seem to form a different race from the rest of mankind."[17]

Empire served as an important source of Britons' pride in themselves and in the principles that they claimed governed their social, economic, cultural, and political institutions. Although it was palpably not the case for all of those people whose liberty and freedom had been sacrificed to the material interests of their British rulers—native Americans, African slaves, Irish Catholic peasants—supporters of empire depicted their enterprise as one in which notions of liberty and consent were central. The ability to portray the colonies as bastions of freedom and liberty for white Britons depended upon the suppression, in real and in imaginative terms, of those who did not and could not enjoy such beneficence. New, scientifically systematized ideologies of race and gender, oftentimes intertwined with one another, served as justifications for the rule of Protestant Britons over subject peoples in Ireland, North America, and the West Indies, and women at home. Portrayed as commercially prosperous colonies inhabited by free white British citizens, the eighteenth-century empire was regarded as the source of trade, wealth, military power, and political virtue for the mother country.

Following the loss of the American colonies in 1783, the British acquired control over significant portions of India. In the years following the Napoleonic wars, Britain established control over huge areas in South Africa, Asia, the West Indies, and Canada. In the decades between 1840 and 1870, it expanded its holdings by adding new colonies in Australia, New Zealand, British Columbia, Hong Kong, Lower Burma, Natal, the Transvaal, parts of what would become Nigeria and Sierra Leone, the Gold Coast, and the Punjab, Sind, Berar, and Oudh in India. While it granted various measures of representative government to the white settlement colonies in Canada, South Africa, Australia, and New Zealand by 1860, it progressively tightened its control over millions of peoples of color. Britain's possession of vast territories in South Asia, Africa, and the West Indies, its rule over the subject peoples inhabiting these areas, and above all, the continued existence of slavery, could not be easily reconciled with liberal principles of constitutionalism, representative government, individual rights, and laissez-faire.

Classical liberalism contained within it a number of potentially incompatible elements, making it possible for individuals of vastly disparate beliefs to band together under its rubric. But liberals of all stripes did share a number of tenets in common that gave the doctrine a coherence that transcended all differences.

Underlying the principles of liberalism as various thinkers understood them was a fundamental belief in the universality of human
nature, and complete faith that the influences of law, education,
and free trade could dramatically transform human beings. These
liberal assumptions about human nature held true for peoples as
far afield as Asia and Africa, and informed liberal approaches to
British imperial rule in the 1830s, 1840s, and early 1850s, especially as it pertained to slavery.

Antislavery activists came to their beliefs from a variety of
philosophic positions. Some radical men and women took a political stand on slavery, seeing it as a violation of fundamental rights
to freedom that all persons enjoyed, regardless of class, race, or
gender. After the outbreak of the French Revolution, and the
revolt of slaves in San Domingo in Haiti in 1791, this particular
strand of antislavery belief lost popularity, certainly among
middle- and upper-class white men and women. Political economists and Utilitarians such as Harriet Martineau saw in slavery
an inefficient use of labor that stood in opposition to principles of
laissez-faire and unnecessarily drove up the cost of commodities.
John Stuart Mill, the preeminent spokesman for classical liberal
thought, objected to slavery on the grounds of justice; he believed
that education could render all men, and, as we shall see in
Chapter 4, women, capable of the reasoning necessary for the exercise of personal freedom. At different times, such perspectives
on antislavery came to the fore, but the single most dominant
strand of antislavery thought derived from evangelical religion.
Slavery was sinful, believed evangelicals of every stripe, a crime
against God's law, and on moral and spiritual grounds, must be
extirpated. Humanitarian sentiments about the cruel fates experienced by other creatures of God often prevailed over more abstract liberal notions of utility, reason, or justice.

Parliament abolished slavery in 1833 because it could no
longer be tolerated by the vast majority of Britons. For a brief
period in the 1820s, 1830s, and 1840s, eighteenth-century notions of absolute racial difference were driven underground by

liberal and humanitarian sentiments expressed through the anti-slavery movement. Britons found slavery incompatible with their sense of rightness, their sense of themselves. To be "British" in the 1830s and 1840s entailed holding an abolitionist position, whether for political, economic, or sentimental reasons, as much as it involved embracing liberalism and the concept of separate spheres for men and women. For British women, antislavery sentiments dovetailed precisely with their purported greater sensitivity to cruelties and injustices, their greater morality and higher spiritual natures. For British men, devotion to Christian precepts as much as to liberal principles of justice and legal equality meant that no respectable middle-class male could turn a blind eye to the brutalities of slavery. Notions of manliness contained a strong element of abolitionism, of ending the oppression of African men, women, and children at the hands of British planters and overlords.[18]

Evangelicals and liberals understood slaves to be part of the human family of man. James Phillippo, a Baptist missionary to Jamaica, asserted that slaves were "men of the same common origin with ourselves,—of the same form and delineation of feature, though with a darker skin,—men endowed with minds equal in dignity, equal in capacity, and equal in duration of experience—men of the same social dispositions and affections, and destined to occupy the same rank with ourselves in the great family of man."[19] The model of a universal human family enabled abolitionists to think in terms of equality before God and to see slavery as an abomination, but this imagined family structure closely resembled that of British families, in which a patriarchal father ruled over his dependent wife and children. Within it, male slaves and men of color more generally—and, indeed, at various historical moments, white workingmen and Irishmen—occupied the position of children, who would have to be guided and educated into manhood, which could not be attained until they enjoyed property in themselves and thus independence. Slave women and women of color required schooling in the ways of separate sphere ideology; they would have to learn to depend upon, serve, and be subservient to their husbands and fathers.

Within the evangelicals' family of man rhetoric, white Britons positioned themselves as older brothers and sisters, teachers and defenders of their younger siblings who needed education in the ways of civilization and morality, reason and domesticity, and protection from the depredations of ungodly planters. Frequently, the language of older brother and sister merged with that of father and mother, so that the hierarchies of power and inequality between whites and people of color might become even more pronounced. "Sons of Africa," "babes in Christ," as black Jamaicans were styled by white missionaries in a relationship of children to parent, "are willing to be taught," noted Willam Knibb, another Baptist missionary, "and where there is sympathy with them, they love those who instruct them." John Candler wrote in 1840 that "the Negroes, with all their shrewdness, have much of the child about them, and need to be humoured." While British men saw themselves as emancipators of the poor and downtrodden in the 1830s and 1840s, they did so in a paternalistic way. Jamaican freemen and women might enjoy the potential for equality with Europeans, but by no means had they attained even a small measure of the qualities that would bring them up to the level of their white saviors. White, but especially English, superiority to people of color had never been called into question by the antislavery campaigners.[20]

Between the early 1830s and the late 1840s, white missionaries focused their efforts in Jamaica on raising black Jamaican men to adulthood as they understood it within their own British context. Phillippo exulted that Christian teachings were helping to eliminate the traits ascribed to Africans, which he saw as a product of slavery. "That cunning, craft, and suspicion—those dark passions and savage dispositions before described as characteristics of the negro," he wrote, "if ever possessed in the degree in which they are attributed to him,—are now giving place to a noble, manly, and independent, yet patient and submissive spirit."

Missionaries looked to create a society among Africans that looked very much like their own at home, complete with its gender sensibilities. Phillippo invoked eighteenth-century notions of a society's progress being measured by the treatment of its women when he noted that after emancipation black Jamaicans, "like the inhabitants of all uncivilized nations, . . . treated the women as inferior in the scale of being to themselves." Men preyed upon young girls, noted Knibb, who sought to establish separate schools for girls where they would be instructed by female teachers in the ways of decency and morality. "I know full well," he declared, "that until the female character is raised, we shall never far advance in civilization and virtue." In later years, both he and Phillippo counted their moral victories by the numbers of couples they had united in marriage and domesticity, judging their success in civilizing black Jamaicans by "the cottager's comfortable home, by the wife's proper release from toil, by the instructed child," as Knibb put it in decidedly English imagery.[21]

Missionaries in Jamaica sought to develop a class and gender system much like that of England's, in which they occupied the role of the prosperous professional middle class and black Jamaicans became part of a free labor force comprised of industrious workers. For black men they sought "a fair day's work for a fair day's wage." For black women who had to earn, domestic service appeared to missionaries to be the most appropriate kind of work for them, for it did not appreciably subvert the emphasis on domesticity for women in that way that work in the fields of a plantation might. "Domestic servants are beginning to be eminently trustworthy," wrote Phillippo approvingly, "and, when properly treated and confided in, do not suffer by comparison with the great bulk of the same class in England." Such progress, he celebrated, indicated that the postemancipation project of raising up a civilized society of black Jamaicans was succeeding, for black Jamaican women were "advancing to that high moral standard which is fixed in the great Christian code." The degree to which black Jamaican families resembled the ideal family of white, middle-class Britons denoted exactly the degree to which they had become civilized.[22]

Liberalism made its triumphant appearance on Britain's home stage with the Reform Act of 1832. It appeared earlier in India, with the arrival in 1828 of Lord William Bentinck as governor-general, who proceeded to implement reforms in law, education, and administration that would excite the envy of liberals at home. Employees of the East India Company, such as John Stuart Mill and Charles Trevelyan, and governmental officials, such as Thomas Macaulay, looked forward with confidence to the day when enlightened and just government, free trade, and education would so change Indian peoples—whom for the most part, like their eighteenth-century predecessors, they regarded as indolent, sensual, wanting in mental liberty and individuality, and in thrall to despotic rule—that they would be ready for self-government. For example, in his "Essay on Robert Clive," the conqueror of Bengal in the 1750s, Macaulay likened Bengali men to women, "enervated by a soft climate and accustomed to peaceful employments." "The physical organization of the Bengalee is feeble even to effeminacy. . . . During many ages he has been trampled upon by men of bolder and more hardy breeds. Courage, independence, veracity are qualities to which his constitution and his situation are equally unfavorable." "There never," he lamented, "perhaps existed a people so thoroughly fitted by habit for a foreign yoke."[23]

But with British examples of firm but just government before them, and education in the ways of British law, thought, and morality, even these poor specimens of manhood could aspire to manly self-rule. "Trained by us to happiness and independence," Trevelyan exclaimed, "India will remain the proudest monument of British benevolence." Macaulay echoed him in a speech in 1833 upon the renewal of the East India Company's charter. India, he noted, might someday, having become instructed in European knowledge, demand European institutions of self-government. Such a development was only to be hoped for, he insisted, and "never will I attempt to avert or retard it. Whenever it comes, it will be the proudest day in English history."[24]

Making self-governing Indians out of the existing population, "sunk in the lowest depths of slavery and superstition," required a wholesale reconstruction of Indian culture and society. Indians would have to be turned into Englishmen, in effect. The evangelical leader of the antislavery movement, William Wilberforce, believed that Anglicizing India constituted the greatest of all causes, exceeding even that of ending slavery. "Let us endeavour to strike our roots into the soil by the gradual introduction and establishment of our own principles and opinions; of our laws, institutions, and manners; above all, as the source of every other improvement, of our religion, and consequently of our morals." As Macaulay's "Minute on Education" put it in 1835, the British must not simply educate a discrete group of Indians in English language and law so that it might help to govern the subcontinent, rather, they must create Indians who were "English in taste, in opinions, in morals and in intellect." Self-governing Indians would be those who had imbibed "our arts and our morals, our literature and our laws." Indeed, in the 1830s and 1840s, the British trained a cadre of Indians, many of them Bengali Hindus, in English literature, law, history, and philosophy. Western in thought and customs, these educated Indians were often more British than the British, whose elites were educated in classical Latin and Greek rather than in English languages and literatures.[25]

Instituting reform of legal procedure, tax collection, land ownership, usage, and tenure, education, and administrative practices proved far easier than implementing religious or cultural change, but efforts to raise Indian morality to a level approximating that of the British proceeded apace nonetheless. These revolved around British outrage at what they considered the degraded state of Indian women at the hands of Indian men, in keeping with the widespread European belief that the treatment of women in any given place provided the measure of its civilization. Closed off and confined in the zenana, covered by the veil,

Indian women, regarded by the British as especially sexual, served as the marker by means of which Indian immorality was gauged. Because Indian men would do nothing to lift up their women to the levels of modesty and purity demanded by domestic ideology, Britons declaimed, it was left to the British to rescue them from their own men.

The practice of sati, or widow burning, offered the most egregious example of Indian savagery to Britons and provides a clear instance of Britons' efforts to erase crucial elements of Indian involvement in its abolition so as to present themselves as heroic defenders of Indian womanhood against Indian men. The spectacle of a living woman being burned to death upon the funeral pyre of her dead husband, despite the relative infrequency with which it took place, excited condemnation among reformers and evangelicals at home and in India. Indians themselves, led by the liberal reformer Ram Mohan Roy, played a central role in the initiative that led Britain to outlaw sati in 1829, but credit for ending what Indians no less than Britons regarded as an abuse of Indian women was laid exclusively in the laps of Britons. A statue of Bentinck, designed by his English supporters to honor his efforts to "elevate the moral and intellectual character" of Indians, stands on a pedestal containing a scene of sati, in which a barebreasted woman, her sari draped down below her hips, is being dragged from her children to the funeral pyre by a man wearing a distinctly phallic sword. Not intrinsically an act containing sexual implications, sati was nevertheless depicted using sexual imagery in order to demonstrate a particularly British highmindedness. The juxtaposition of a sexualized woman and the violence of sword and fire, over which stood the man, Bentinck, responsible for "abolishing cruel rites," served as a vivid illustration of Britain's superior morality to an uncivilized, unmanly people steeped in blood and barbarism. Liberals and evangelicals could dramatically demonstrate their own manliness and civilization by stamping out such ungodly practices and bringing enlightened, Christian, liberal reforms in their wake.

The years of Victoria's childhood, which she experienced personally as a time of confinement and stultifying suffocation at the hands of her mother and Lord Conroy, saw dramatic changes in the political, social, and economic realms of Britain and its imperial possessions. The transformations in the political and social realms, in particular, would create paradoxes and contradictions that Victoria would have to learn to negotiate and finesse, processes that did not always go smoothly, as we shall see in the next chapter.

CHAPTER 2

QUEEN, WIFE, MOTHER: SEPARATE SPHERE IDEOLOGY AND THE PARADOX OF FEMALE MONARCHY, 1840–1861

EARLY ON THE MORNING OF JUNE 20, 1837, the Archbishop of Canterbury and the Lord Chamberlain arrived at Kensington Palace to inform Victoria that her uncle, King William IV, had died and to swear allegiance to her as their new monarch. It was the first time she had met with anyone without her mother, Conroy, or one of their agents present, and it marked the end of Victoria's enforced isolation from the world around her. She moved quickly to demolish the "Kensington system," meeting that morning "quite alone," as she had insisted, with the privy council to formally declare the transfer of power. Though young and small of stature, standing less than five feet tall, Victoria impressed the privy councilors with her poise and command. "She not merely filled her chair," the Duke of Wellington remarked, "she filled the room."[1] Within a month of her accession, Victoria had moved her court to Buckingham Palace, where she settled her mother in apartments far from her own quarters and refused to give Conroy a household appointment.

Poised and determined though she was to exercise her own will, Victoria was nevertheless inexperienced in the ways of royal

Queen Victoria's First Council, 1837.

etiquette regarding her political status. She turned immediately to the Whig prime minister at the time, Lord Melbourne, for guidance. In him, she found not just an advisor but also the father figure she had never had; he, forty years her senior, discovered in the young queen a daughter to fill the hole created by the deaths of his wife and his only child, a son. She became dependent upon him not only for political counsel but also for education in all manner of things, advice about comportment and dress, gossip concerning current and former eminences, dinner conversation, and companionship. When the general election occasioned by Victoria's accession returned a Whig majority of only forty in the House of Commons in November 1837, Melbourne's tenure became precarious, a situation that caused Victoria great anxiety lest his government fall.

As we have seen, Victoria became queen in the midst of a transformation of Britain's social, economic, and political structures. Once a system characterized by ranks and orders, in which landed and commercial elites whose wealth derived from agriculture and commerce monopolized political power, it gave way to

Queen Victoria and Lord Melbourne, 1838.

one in which frequently mutually antagonistic classes vied with one another for political power within an economic system dominated by industry. In virtually every one of the political showdowns—first between middle-class men and aristocrats, and then between middle-class men and plebeians—the arguments for and against inclusion in the political life of the nation rested upon one's fitness to rule; fitness being construed as sober, serious, respectable men possessing virtuous women who restricted themselves to the domestic sphere.

Working-class radicals, whose efforts to gain the right to vote continued long after their betrayal by former middle-class allies in 1832 in a movement known as Chartism, refused to cede to the middle classes an exclusive claim to domesticity and separate spheres. Although it would take more than a century for the majority of working-class families to attain the financial status necessary to actually implement an arrangement of separate spheres for men and women, the ideal of the male breadwinner and the stay-at-home wife and mother took hold among many working people before mid-century, and would serve to justify in the minds of political elites the enfranchisement of urban working-class men in 1867. Male agricultural workers won the vote in 1884, so that by the end of the nineteenth century, a parliamentary democracy of men (women would not be enfranchised until 1918, and then only partially) can be said to have been established. The process of moving to a parliamentary democracy meant that the British monarchy, no matter who occupied the throne, would undergo dramatic changes in the way it operated. No longer a state power in its own right, the monarchy took on a symbolic role.

What, under these circumstances, did it mean to be a monarch in the nineteenth century?

The revolutionary settlement following the Glorious Revolution of 1688 established a constitutional monarchy in England and Wales (and later Scotland and Ireland), checking the power of monarchs and placing significant authority in the hands of the landed elites who sat in parliament. Monarchs still played an important role in governance. They acted as commanders in chief of the armed forces and could declare or end wars and negotiate peace treaties; they appointed the important ministers of state, governors of British colonies, and the men who sat on the high court; they could ennoble commoners and make them hereditary peers of the realm, thus creating a body of presumably friendly men who sat for life in the House of Lords; they could request that parliament consider legislation or the appropriation of funds necessary to administer and defend Britain; and, as heads of the Anglican church, they designated the bishops and archbishops who served the Church of England and the Church of Ireland. But for over a hundred years prior to Victoria's succession to the throne, these powers had largely been carried out by the prime minister and his cabinet. Certainly, monarchs expected to be briefed and their opinions solicited before any policies were arrived at or actions taken. And, perhaps most important, monarchs guarded their prerogative to appoint—and dismiss—the prime minister in the first place, though the strength of the majority party in parliament, and especially in the House of Commons, often dictated the outcome, despite the monarch's wishes.

In fact, for a number of decades before Victoria's accession, the authority of the crown had been diminished relative to that of parliament, a process that we might regard as the feminization of the monarchy. The debauchery, profligacy, and excesses of George IV had badly damaged the prestige of the crown. We have seen how aristocrats had become associated with effeminacy in the late eighteenth and early nineteenth centuries; George's antics confirmed contemporaries in those beliefs. The efforts of his brother, William IV, to impress his political will on parliament had come to naught. He had been unable to block significant reform measures championed by the Whigs, and his 1834 dismissal of the Whig government under Lord Melbourne would, though no one knew it at the time, prove to be the last such action on the part of any monarch. Nor could William keep the Tories he appointed to power in office for very long—another indication that the crown had been significantly weakened. Moreover, in a symbolic contestation of monarchy versus parliament, the royal court suffered from the fact that it had never been an exclusively masculine site—women had always been present at court, regardless of the gender of the ruler on the throne. Parliament, by contrast, had always only been male, and it would not surrender its gender exclusivity until 1918. The arrival of Victoria on the throne rendered concrete what had earlier been symbolic—a female monarch now embodied the loss of power relative to parliament that had been taking place for almost fifty years.[2]

The fact of Victoria's regnancy constituted a troubling paradox. Liberalism, as we saw articulated clearly in James Mill's writings and in the wording of the Reform Act of 1832, explicitly denied women political citizenship. The potential contradiction between, on the one hand, a liberal ideology that had legitimated the dismantling of aristocratic power and authority and the enfranchisement of middle-class, and later working-class, men and, on the other, the denial of the claims of women to full citizenship was resolved by appeals to biological and characterological differences between the sexes. Definitions of femininity evolved whose qualities were antithetical to those that had warranted widespread male participation in the public sphere. Men possessed the capacity for reason, action, aggression, independence, and self-interest. Women inhabited a separate, private sphere, one suitable for the so-called inherent qualities of femininity: emotion, passivity, submission, dependence, and selflessness, all derived, it was claimed insistently, from women's sexual and reproductive organization. Upon the female as a biological entity, a sexed body, nineteenth-century theorists imposed a socially and culturally constructed femininity, a gender identity derived from ideas about what roles were appropriate for women. This collapsing of sex and gender—of the physiological organism with the normative social creation—made it possible for women to be construed as at once pure and purely sexual; although paradoxically, these definitions excluded women from participation in the public sphere and rendered them subordinate to men in the private sphere as well.

These arguments at one and the same time idealized women and expressed profound fear of them. On the one hand, women were aligned with morality and religion, whereas men represented corruption and materialism. Women were construed as occupying the ethical center of industrial society, invested with the guardianship of social values, whereas men functioned in a world of shady dealings, greed, and vice, values generally subversive of a civilized order. On the other hand, women were also identified with nature—wild, unruly, yet to be explored and mastered; whereas men belonged to culture—controlled, systematic, symbolic of achievement and order. Correspondingly, women were assigned an exclusively reproductive function, in contrast to men, who allegedly held a monopoly on productivity. In each case, notions of femininity, or female nature, ultimately rested upon the perceived sexual organization of women, who were construed to be either sexually comatose or helplessly nymphomaniacal. Whether belonging to one category or the other, women were so exclusively identified by their sexual functions that nineteenth-century society came to regard them as "the Sex." This in turn set up yet another dichotomy, which offered two possible images for women: that of revered wife and mother, or that of despised prostitute. Both roles effectively disqualified women from economic and political activity.

Where did Victoria fit in all this? Certainly, her position was wildly at odds with the law as it pertained to every woman other than herself. She, alone among her sex, did not fall under the constraints of coverture as established by common law; she was subject only to the British constitution. Lord Brougham, a radical, pointed up the anomaly of the young queen in an anonymous pamphlet. "An experienced man, well stricken in years," he complained:

> I hold myself before you, a girl of eighteen, who, in my own or any other family in Europe, would be treated as a child, ordered to do as was most agreeable or convenient to others—whose inclinations would never be consulted—whose opinions would never be thought of—whose consent would never be asked upon any one thing appertaining to any other human being but yourself, beyond the choice of gown or cap, nor always that: yet before you I humble myself.[3]

Two incidents provide us with striking examples of the contradictions created by the presence of a queen on the throne in a social system informed by the ideology of separate spheres. The so-called bedchamber crisis occurred in May 1839, when Lord Melbourne's government resigned after its majority in the House of Commons fell to five during a vote on the Jamaica Bill, which would end self-government there and return the island to direct rule under the crown. Bereft over losing her faithful and beloved friend and servant, and despairing at the prospect of having to approve a Tory government, Victoria staged a confrontation with Sir Robert Peel, leader of the Tory party, over the composition of her ladies of the bedchamber. The women holding these positions had long served as attendants to the queen, but they had also become political appointments, given out to the wives, daughters, and sisters of prominent personages in the government. Convention had come to dictate that when governments changed, the ladies would as well, reflecting the realities of the shift in power. Sir Robert Peel, insecure in his position because he did not enjoy a majority in parliament, sought an expression of the queen's confidence in him by asking her to replace some of her Whig ladies-in-waiting with Tory ladies. Victoria refused him outright, ultimately forcing Peel to back down and to withdraw his proposal to form a new government, and returning the Whigs under Lord Melbourne to power.

Victoria objected to Peel's request to change her ladies on at least two grounds. She did not like the Tory leader, and the thought of losing Melbourne nearly panicked her; she believed that by holding firm against Peel she could bring about a reversal of Melbourne's fortunes. But she also insisted that her power would not be diminished. She wrote to Melbourne that she "felt this was an attempt to see whether she could be led and managed like a child." She "has only been defending her own rights," she told him, "on a point which so nearly concerned her person, and which, if they had succeeded in, would have led to every sort of unfair attempt at power." She prevailed, but in doing so she advanced arguments that had the paradoxical effect of undermining her power. In her rebuttal to Peel's observation that her ladies "were the wives of the opponents of the Government," Victoria asserted that the ladies "would not interfere; that I never talked politics with them." She declared that never had such a demand been made of a queen, to which Peel replied that her status as queen regnant, rather than queen consort, made all the difference in this instance. "Not here," she responded, "and I maintained my right."[4]

Victoria's stance in this showdown proved ultimately victorious, but at great cost to the nature of her authority. First, her insistence that she never talked politics with her ladies implied that her private world remained separate and apart from considerations or relations of power. In effect, it reduced the realm of her power. Secondly, by invoking the right of queens to maintain their choices of household appointments, she equated her position as a regnant queen to that of queen consorts—the wives of kings, who held no sovereignty. She demoted herself, in other words, to the level of consort by comparing her situation with that of earlier queens. As one biographer has noted, Victoria "was able to assert her authority only by giving up some aspect of it."[5]

Another incident in which Victoria involved herself produced the same effect. This one concerned a close associate of her mother's, Lady Flora Hastings, who in the first months of 1839 began to show a swelling of her abdomen. Lady Flora had recently voyaged from Scotland with the hated Sir John Conroy, and Victoria and her ladies seized upon the two circumstances to circulate rumors that the unmarried Lady Flora was pregnant. It soon emerged that she was not, but not before her brother issued a public broadside against the court and called for the dismissal of the queen's intimate, Baroness Lehzen. When Lady Flora died from abdominal cancer in July, the outcry against the queen grew louder. When she appeared in public, audiences hissed at her.

Victoria's rumor mongering had been directed against the authority of her mother, the Duchess of Kent, who justified her continued presence at court by insisting that the unmarried young queen required a chaperone. Victoria resented her and wished her away, but propriety dictated that she must stay. Melbourne reminded the queen that if her mother would remain until she found a husband, "well, then, there's *that* way of settling it." In other words, the only way Victoria could assert her independence from her mother would be to take a husband, to whom she would be expected by law and by social custom to be subordinate.

Victoria did not want a husband, fearing that marriage would undermine her sovereign power. As she had put it in April 1839, "my feeling was quite against ever marrying. . . . I observed that marrying a subject was making yourself so much their equal. . . . I was so accustomed to have my own way."[6] She could see no reason "why [I] need . . . marry at all for 3 or 4 years."[7] But the Lady Flora affair, along with the bedchamber crisis, convinced many contemporaries that "it was about time that the Queen was freed from her female entourage, and had the protective advice of a husband."[8] When she told Melbourne again in July that she "wished if possible never to marry," he replied, "I don't know about that."[9] Victoria's deep desire to rid herself of her mother's control combined with the public's fears of female rule to make marriage the most obvious way out of her personal and political dilemma. Before long, the young queen identified a suitable prospect: her cousin Prince Albert of Saxe-Coburg and Gotha, whom she married in February 1840.

THE QUEEN'S MARRIAGE TO PRINCE ALBERT, IN THE CHAPEL OF ST. JAMES'S PALACE, FEB. 10, 1840.
After the Picture by Sir George Hayter, R.A.; Engraved by permission of Messrs. H. Graves and Co.

Marriage of Queen Victoria and Prince Albert, 1840.

By marrying, Victoria achieved two ends: she escaped the *"torture!"* as she described it, of living with her mother,[10] and she cemented in the minds of her subjects the image of the monarchy as middle-class and domestic. She presented herself as the quint-essential wife and mother, ensuring the survival of monarchy and even enhancing its prestige. At a time when monarchies all over Europe fell before the forces of revolution, Queen Victoria not only lasted, she thrived, inhabiting a throne that by the end of her reign had lost state power but had gained extraordinary symbolic power. She effected this feat by presenting herself not as a prince presiding over her subjects but as a wife and mother ruling as a woman. Rather than appearing at state occasions in a crown and royal robes, for example, she wore a bonnet and lace. She pro-duced nine children, and consistently presented the royal family in imagery consonant with the values associated with domestic-ity. In a neat correlation between the status of monarchy in a system converting to parliamentary democracy and that of a middle-class woman inhabiting the private sphere assigned to her by separate sphere ideology, Victoria came to inhabit the per-sonae and display the characteristics of both: passivity, duty, and moral power or influence. As one critic has put it,

> Just like a middle-class wife, the monarch was obliged (since the seventeenth century, but increasingly so) not to intervene in poli-tics. Like a middle-class wife spending her husband's income, she had to spend the wealth of her nation in a manner that displayed both its economic prowess and her dependency; she had to be the chief consumer in a nation of consumers. And she had to serve as a public, highly visible symbol of national identity and of her na-tion's values, just as a middle-class wife might be expected to dis-play her husband's status.[11]

Victoria pulled off this act with great effectiveness, leaving the throne with far greater international and domestic prestige than it had enjoyed at the beginning of her reign. This act did not start out smoothly, however. Victoria, as we have seen, did not want to marry, and did so planning to hold on to all the trappings of her power. She enjoyed the work devolved upon her as queen and had no inclination to share or give it over to anyone else. Albert, on the other hand, approached marriage determined to assert as much traditional male power over his wife as he could. The clash between these two agendas could not be reconciled, and for a year following their engagement in October 1839, the tensions they created were often severe. Victoria sought to build up Albert's public position as much as she could but was thwarted in many of her efforts by parliament, whose members, Whig and Tory alike, did not like the fact that Albert was foreign and suspected his motives in marrying. Lord Melbourne refused to consider the suggestion that Albert be made a duke and dismissed out of hand Victoria's request that he ask parliament to confer the title of king consort upon the prince. Parliament also declined to settle upon Albert the traditional £50,000 a year allowance granted to spouses of royals, instead conferring only £30,000 on the pretext that the economic distress facing the nation required that government expenditures be reduced.

Despite her initial reluctance to marry, Victoria fell deeply in love with Albert. He did not share the same depth of feeling for her, though he remained an attentive and dutiful husband. She sought to build him up, at least in official ways. What was in Victoria's power alone to do, she did, giving Albert precedence, after herself, over everyone else in the country, to the outrage of her mother and her uncles. She appointed him as a field marshal in the army and conferred the Order of the Garter on him. But the problem for Albert was that he did not accrue these honors and positions by earning them or by virtue of his masculine prerogatives, but because Victoria—his wife—had the power to grant them to him. He felt small and humiliated. The blows to his masculine pride continued after the marriage ceremony: Albert had pushed for a two-week honeymoon, but Victoria informed him haughtily that the queen could not possibly be away from her duties and responsibilities for more than three days. When the couple returned to Buckingham Palace, Victoria resumed her work, seeing her ministers alone and refusing to admit Albert to any official business beyond blotting her signature on state papers. The situation rankled, and the prince wrote to a friend that he was not "master in his house," a position he found intolerable. He could only conclude that his wife had been "warped by wrong upbringing."[12] He expressed his displeasure in childish, passive-aggressive ways, falling asleep at the theater or in the presence of friends and important personages after dinner, going to bed early without his wife, displaying contempt for the English aristocracy, and tearfully complaining to Victoria about his lack of German friends and associates.

Despite Albert's pique at being upstaged by his royal bride, he and Victoria shared a happy and active sex life. We find this sexual compatibility and even eroticism on Victoria's part surprising, as conventional wisdom has held that Victoria gave her name to a period in which prudery in sexual matters prevailed. Indeed, domestic ideology invested in women the responsibility of maintaining morality and purity. "The angel in the house," as the ideology had it, was herself pure, without sexual feeling, passionless. Until the early eighteenth century, contemporaries believed that women's lust, as personified by Eve, was insatiable, but that women could become spiritual through God's grace, and hence less carnal. During the eighteenth and nineteenth centuries, the dominant definition of women as especially sexual was reversed and transformed into the view that women were less carnal and less lustful than men. The notion of the woman without passion came into being. Passionlessness was, in the eighteenth century, a product of women's purported superior moral and spiritual nature, and it helped to give women a higher status in society than they had enjoyed before. It undermined the identification of women with sexual treachery, and it countered the notion that women were primarily sexual creatures at a time when their social, political, and economic disabilities rendered them vulnerable to predation.

In its early manifestations, passionlessness seemed to offer positive rewards for women; women had a stake in its creation as an ideology and its acceptance and perpetuation by society. As physicians took up the notion of passionlessness in the mid-nineteenth century, however, they reduced it from its moral and spiritual connotations to a phenomenon involving scientific, biological principles. Their version of the passionlessness of women once again imposed an exclusively sexual characterization upon them; it placed them in a position of sexual vulnerability while at the same time justifying anew their exclusion from traditionally male pursuits.

In denying middle-class women sexuality, nineteenth-century bourgeois society paradoxically heightened an awareness of women as primarily reproductive and sexual beings. One aspect of the physicians' science of sex insisted upon women's utter lack of sexual feeling; the other asserted that women's bodies were saturated with sex. William Acton, in *Functions and Disorders of the Reproductive Organs*, published in 1857, declared that

> the majority of women (happily for society) are not very much troubled with sexual feeling of any kind. What men are habitually, women are only exceptionally. . . . There can be no doubt that sexual feeling in the female is in the majority of cases in abeyance, and that it requires positive and considerable excitement to be roused at all; and even if aroused (which in many cases it can never be) it is very moderate compared with that of the male.

Acton believed that women's "indifference to sex was naturally ordained to prevent the male's vital energies from being overly expended at any one time."[13]

Not all British physicians accepted Acton's dictum concerning female sexuality. Dr. George Drysdale, for one, believed that sexual pleasure was natural and beneficial to both sexes. In *The Elements of Social Science* (1859), he advocated more frequent sexual intercourse for married couples as a means to prevent disease. Of the inherent purity of the female, Drysdale wrote, "if we examine the origins and meaning of these singular ideas with regard to women, we shall find that they are based upon no natural distinction between sexes, but upon the erroneous views of man, and especially upon the mistaken ideas as to the virtue of female *chastity*."[14] But Drysdale was a man ahead of his time. Acton's views of female sexuality rather than Drysdale's prevailed throughout both the medical profession and society as a whole.

In asserting the nonsexuality of women, doctors helped to encourage the establishment of prudery in social interactions among the middle classes, and he encouraged the idea that ignorance of sexual matters was tantamount to innocence in sexual matters. They encouraged the development of a situation in which women had little or no knowledge of their sexual and reproductive functions. Moreover, the definition of women as pure and asexual, while men remained passionate and lustful, set up a potentially antagonistic relationship between men and women in which men were understood to be aggressive and women to be victimized by that aggression.

Victorian ideology finally offered only two possible images for women. They might be either the idealized wife and mother, the angel in the house, or the debased, depraved, corrupt prostitute. The image of the respectable, passionless middle-class lady, in fact, depended upon a contrast with the other image of the fallen woman. In his discussion of pure women in *Functions and Disorders of the Reproductive Organs*, for instance, Acton asserted that motherhood provided the only motivation for women's sexual activity, whereas natural desire propelled men. "There are many females," he claimed, "who never feel any sexual excitement whatever. . . . Many of the best mothers, wives, and managers of households, know little or are careless about sexual indulgences. Love of home, of children, and of domestic duties are the only passions they feel." While desiring little or no sexual gratification for herself, the modest woman "submits to her husband's embraces, but principally to gratify him; and, were it not for the desire of maternity, would far rather be relieved of his attentions." Some women "evinced positive loathing for any marital familiarity whatever." In such cases, Acton stated, "feeling has been sacrificed to duty, and the wife has endured, with all the self-martyrdom of womanhood, what was almost worse than death." Other women, "who, either from ignorance or utter want of sympathy . . . not only evince no sexual feeling, but, on the contrary, scruple not to declare their aversion to the least manifestation of it." Men who found themselves married to such women complained, "and I think with reason," Acton reported, "that they are debarred from the privileges of marriage, and that their sexual sufferings are almost greater than they can bear in consequence of being mated to women who think and act in the above-cited instances." He warned readers that lack of a sexual outlet "might be . . . highly detrimental to the health of the husband," a problem "ultimately too often ending in impotence."[15]

Like many other women of the period, Victoria went to her marriage bed anxious and unprepared for the "shock" of "the marital act," as she told her daughter Vicky many years later. But the shock soon wore off and she and Albert spent their first night together establishing an erotic relationship that would endure throughout much of their marriage. "I never, never spent such an evening," Victoria confided to her journal. "He called me names of tenderness, I have never yet heard used to me before—was bliss beyond belief! Oh! This was the happiest day of my life!" When she awoke the next morning—"we did not sleep much" that night, the queen noted—she gazed upon "that beautiful angelic face by my side, it was more than I can express!" She marveled at her husband, "so beautiful in his shirt only, with his beautiful throat seen." Clearly, they had successfully and even rapturously consummated their marriage, and Victoria reveled in the physical intimacy she found with Albert: on the last day of their honeymoon, "my dearest Albert put on my stockings for me. I went in and saw him shave; a great delight for me."[16] Victoria insisted that she and Albert sleep together every night. She possessed, as she admitted to Vicky, a "warm passionate loving nature" that required erotic fulfillment. Upon being told by her doctor after the birth of her last child that she should have no more children, she is said to have protested, "Oh Doctor, can I have no more fun in bed?" It turns out that Albert was the prude, not Victoria. When he died, Victoria, only forty-two years old at the time, found it extremely difficult to deal with "the never quenched flame" of desire that could find no outlet. It "burns within me and wears me out!" she lamented.[17]

But if Victoria loved sex, she hated pregnancy and child-birth. Within a week of returning from their honeymoon, Victoria began to experience morning sickness and soon discovered that she was pregnant. Enraged at having been "caught" in this way, she railed against her "unhappy condition."[18] Not only would this mean a premature end to the erotic pleasures she had discovered with her husband, but the discomforts of pregnancy and the dangers of childhood loomed over the next number of months. At the very least, convention held that Victoria could no longer go racing across the countryside on horseback or dance till dawn, as she had since she became queen, and when she could no longer hide her pregnancy, she would have to remove herself from society; more seriously, the prospects of dying in childbirth were not inconsiderable.

For Albert, Victoria's pregnancy proved a boon. Not only had he sired an heir to the throne, but his position vis à vis his wife changed dramatically. Parliament named him sole regent in the event that Victoria died after giving birth, an act that outraged her uncles, who had sought that position for themselves, and signaled a victory for the prince. When the queen opened parliament in June, Albert sat on a throne by her side; and in August, Victoria began to include Albert in the process of going through the documents that appeared on her desk each day. When he showed talent for handling the paperwork efficiently, she provided him with his own key to the dispatch box and appointed him to the privy council. And he stood in for the queen when her pregnancy prevented her from appearing in public. He was delighted, writing to his advisor, Baron Stockmar, "I have come to be extremely pleased with Victoria during the last few months. She . . . puts more confidence in me daily."[19]

The discomforts and inconveniences of pregnancy made Victoria dependent upon her husband. He responded magnificently, attending to her every need, carrying her from one place to another, looking after her health and physical condition, and, when the time came, staying with her throughout the twelve-hour labor. Custom dictated against a husband attending his wife's confinement, but Albert paid it no mind; he comforted the queen and was there when a girl child, named Victoria Adelaide Mary Louisa, was delivered on November 21, 1840. Told it was a girl, Victoria replied, "Never mind, the next will be a prince."[20]

As indeed it was. Bertie, the baby who would be the heir to the throne, arrived less than a year after Vicky's birth. If the first pregnancy distressed Victoria, the second, taking place so soon after the first, infuriated her. She had written to King Leopold earlier that "men never think, at least seldom think, what a hard task it is for us women to go through this *very often*." She suffered more severely through her second pregnancy and the labor was longer and more painful; after Bertie's birth, she fell into a prolonged depression. She later protested to Vicky against the misery she underwent in bearing four children in the first four years of marriage. "One becomes so worn out and one's nerves so miserable," she complained. "The poor woman is bodily and morally the husband's slave. That always sticks in my throat. When I think of a merry happy free young girl—and look at the ailing, aching state a young wife is generally doomed to, which you can't deny is the penalty of marriage." The physical debility she experienced, the "aches—and sufferings and miseries and plagues . . . and enjoyments, etc. to give up"—for all these travails, "I think our sex a most unenviable one," she told Vicky at another time.[21]

Victoria incurred that penalty seven more times, producing Alice in 1843, Alfred in 1844, Helena in 1846, Louise in 1848,

Arthur in 1850, Leopold in 1853, and Beatrice in 1857. The queen loved sex, slept with her husband frequently, had no access to birth control information, and knew nothing about erotic practices that would not result in pregnancy. Contraceptive methods existed, but they were generally associated with debauched libertines and prostitutes, and it would have been difficult to keep rumors about them from spreading throughout the royal household. One presumes, knowing what we do about her attitude toward sexuality, that Victoria would not have been adverse to nonreproductive sex, but she would have had to rely upon Albert, who grew more and more prudish each year, to learn of them, and that was unlikely to happen. So, pregnancy and childbearing it was, to her deep dismay.

For the birth of her eighth child, Victoria asked that chloroform be administered to help her deal with the pain. She had learned of its existence from her physician, who told her that a number of physicians were experimenting with it. Eager to lessen her travail, the queen determined to use it, despite the fact that many prominent doctors and clergymen advised against it. The clergy regarded the pain of childbirth as God's punishment for Eve's transgressions in the Garden of Eden, and believed that circumventing divine wrath constituted a sin. Doctors declared that they had watched as respectable wives under the influence of chloroform or ether turned into shameless hussies who made sexual advances to their physicians. Victoria was not swayed by their arguments and scare tactics, and when she began the last stages of labor, Dr. John Snow periodically dosed her with chloroform by pouring small amounts on a handkerchief and holding it against her nose. It worked, and Victoria pronounced herself grateful for the decrease in pain she suffered during that labor. Overnight the strictures against the use of chloroform fell away: The queen's imprimatur on the practice made it possible for generations of subsequent women to ask for the anesthetic without being made to feel they were sinful or monstrous for using it.

Queen Victoria with Albert and their family, 1860.

Incredibly for the time, Victoria never miscarried nor lost a child, and she herself seems to have recovered her health after each birth. All nine children survived into adulthood, though Leopold, who inherited the hemophilia gene carried by his mother, passed a painful and difficult childhood. Victoria did not care much for her children, excepting Vicky, disdaining them as babies and finding them disappointing as they grew older and turned out to have opinions and wills different from those of their parents. This most domestic of queens, the nation's exemplary and beloved mother, merely tolerated her children, and sometimes not even that. She resented the time they took away from being alone with her husband.

Albert, on the other hand, rejoiced in them, delighting in fatherhood and devoting hours to them. He flew kites with the children, played hide-and-seek, took them on outings to the zoo and the circus, and read to them before bed. His attention to the children provoked Victoria's jealousy; she wrote later that "I often grudged you children being always there, when I longed to be alone with dearest Papa!"[22]

Albert delighted even more in the role that his wife's constant pregnancies thrust upon him. For the queen had, perforce, to give over much of her authority in official matters to her husband while she was pregnant. Melbourne's government fell in the summer of 1841, and Victoria, pregnant with her second child, turned to Albert to take his place as private secretary and advisor. This he did with alacrity, reading every document that came across the queen's desk, attending her meetings with ministers, corresponding with ministers in his own name and frequently dictating the messages sent in hers. He wrote policy papers and maintained a correspondence with the most important men in Britain and on the continent. When, in 1842, he succeeded in removing Baroness Lehzen from the family after a metaphoric knock-down-drag-out fight with the queen, Albert assumed complete control over the household—finances, care and education of the children, and mastery over his wife. He had won the battle of domination begun when the two married, and Victoria pronounced herself content with the outcome. She was, she declared, the happiest and most fortunate woman in the world, all owing to her having married the perfect Albert.

Over the next nineteen years, Albert acted as co-ruler with Victoria. Few people knew about this, for he was careful always to preserve her prerogative, but Lord Charles Grenville, an astute observer of the period, professed astonishment at the degree to which the prince had asserted control. They "are one person," he confided to his diary, "and as he likes and she dislikes business, it is obvious that while she has the title, he is really discharging the functions of the Sovereign. He is King to all intents and purposes."[23] Victoria had not abdicated her power, and she determined still to reign as queen, but she trusted Albert to carry out the business of monarchy efficiently and effectively, as indeed he did. They ruled together, for all intents and purposes; indeed, starting in 1842, the queen began to use the term "we" in her letters, diary, and conversation. It wasn't the so-called royal we that virtually all her predecessors had used to signal their supremacy over all others; it indicated quite literally the partnership she enjoyed with her husband in ruling Britain and the empire.

Fully in charge now as his wife gave her life over to seemingly endless pregnancies, Albert turned to imposing a regime of morality upon the royal household that would characterize life at court for the rest of Victoria's reign. We have come to think of the Victorian period as one in which prudery in sexual matters reached ludicrous proportions and have attributed that development to the queen who gave her name to the period. In fact, Albert, not Victoria, demanded that the behavior of all who came into contact with the queen and their children should be flawless and insisted that no one who had even the slightest mention of impropriety attached to his or her name should be admitted to the queen's presence. This meant that members of Victoria's immediate family—aunts, uncles, and cousins—were no longer welcome at court owing to the reputations for all kinds of excesses they had acquired over the course of their lives. Closer to home, the members of the royal household were held to a standard of behavior never known till now: any hint of improper behavior resulted in immediate dismissal. Young ladies-in-waiting to the queen had to be chaperoned by older attendants; neither they nor the men of the household were allowed to walk about the grounds of Buckingham Palace during their off-hours so that no opportunity for secret love affairs might arise. Under the watchful eyes and ears of the prince, parties and dinners became dull, tedious affairs in which conversation lagged and attendees counted the minutes left before they could leave. The contrast to the days of George IV could not have been more striking, as lavish parties, raucous behavior, and scandals of all kinds at court gave way to boring and strictly controlled events. The royal family increasingly retreated from public view, except in the most carefully contrived circumstances, establishing itself as a private entity where parents and children lived happily, lovingly, and respectably together.

Although the elites of Britain might grumble at the offenses committed against their fun-loving, lascivious, and dissolute life-styles, the middle- and working-class people of the country approved of the changes. Under the influence of evangelicalism, as we have seen, the values associated with the aristocracy had come under severe attack. In fact, Victoria and Albert's commitment to what would come to be seen as a middle-class sensibility, in which sobriety, thrift, strict sexual restraint, responsibility, and hard work prevailed, very likely saved the institution of the monarchy in Britain. The unlovely behavior of previous royals had brought the monarchy into such disrepute that its very existence was called into question. Victoria and Albert, living a life of purpose, rectitude, and domesticity, provided the British people a picture of monarchy in which they could take pride. Victoria's popularity soared; she herself basked in the warmth of her people's affection, demonstrations of which she received everywhere she traveled. In contrast to monarchs on the continent, who were losing their thrones on a regular basis it seemed, Queen Victoria only increased her hold on her subjects' loyalty. Albert, however despised by the upper classes within and without the royal court, had made that possible.

And despised he was, as his moral regime became more and more insufferable. Victoria might be respectable and responsible, but she did not share her husband's prudery or his sanctimonious, judgmental insistence on purity of character, which only increased and indeed became irrational as he grew older. Albert had few friends, and none of them among the men who held the reins of power in the kingdom. When in 1853 he found himself vilified in the press for having overstepped his political bounds, no one in government came to his relief. He found himself humiliatingly dependent upon his wife once again, forced to acknowledge his subsidiary position as prince to her queen. A queen, moreover, who found it difficult to recognize her own constitutional limitations, as we saw in the affair of the bedchamber, and who was encouraged in her royal prerogatives vis à vis parliament by her husband.

Victoria and Albert were careful not to step on too many parliamentary toes in the conduct of domestic affairs: though they insisted upon being involved in virtually every development undertaken by the government, they refrained from issuing *diktats* about policy. In foreign affairs, however, they exercised none of these restraints, seeing diplomacy as a special strength of Albert's and interjecting themselves wherever they felt inclined to do so. As a result, they found themselves in an out-and-out war with Lord Palmerston, the foreign secretary. When Palmerston made himself vulnerable by recognizing the government of Louis Napoleon in 1851 without having informed either the prime minister or the queen ahead of time, he was sacked. "Pam," as he was called with great affection by the British populace, made it known that the prince, after years of trying to impose himself over the foreign office, had finally won. A whispering campaign charging the foreign Albert with treason ensued and became louder and more vociferous with each passing year.

In 1853, Russia declared war on Turkey in an effort to gain domination over the Black Sea. A retrogressive autocracy, Russia was regarded by the British people as an anathema, the complete negation of all things liberal. Neither the British government under Lord Aberdeen nor Victoria and Albert wanted war, but the British public clamored for it, seeing an opportunity to revisit the glory years of the Napoleonic wars. When the government refused to declare war on Russia after it defeated the Turkish navy, the public erupted in fury against Albert the foreigner, seeing him as an agent of the tsar who sought to prevent the carrying out of the electorate's wishes. Press accounts picked up and proliferated these tales of princely usurpation of monarchical power, which no politician felt compelled to counteract. "For the last three weeks there have been vile attacks in the newspapers against my dear husband," the queen wrote to Princess Augusta of Prussia, "who is accused of intriguing in the interests of Russia! They are quite mad, and although such nonsense gains no credit among sensible people who respect and love Albert, yet they have provided an occasion for many dreadful remarks, and the whole affair will probably continue until notice is taken of it in Parliament. . . . You will easily understand how enraged and indignant I feel about it."[24]

Furious, Victoria demanded that the government come to Albert's defense. It did so, conducting a special debate in the House of Commons in which the prince's loyalty, unselfishness, and invaluable contributions to the welfare of the nation were hailed by Whig and Tory alike. Parliament had been brought to heel in the matter of smearing the prince, but only because Victoria had ridden in on her charger to compel it to do so. Albert's attempts to dominate foreign affairs, however, had been unmistakably thwarted by the public reaction against him, and he suffered a blow to his ambitions and his pride from which he never recovered. Humiliated by the public, politicians, and by the necessity of relying upon his wife for his defense, Albert found himself, as in the early days of his marriage, forced to bow before her power.

For her part, Victoria relished taking up the reins again. Britain did go to war against Russia in the Crimea in 1854, a conflict that provided the queen with the opportunity to show herself once again to her people. Her pregnancies had kept her out of the public eye for quite some time, but now, as commander in chief of the armed forces, Victoria threw herself into the prosecution of the war with vigor, reviewing the troops clad in full dress uniform and on horseback, visiting hospitals and barracks, awarding medals to her beloved soldiers, and publicly celebrating hard-won victories. In the process, she won back the love of her people, as a letter to her uncle Leopold suggests. "The last battalion of the Guards (Scots Fusiliers) embarked to-day," she wrote in February 1854. "They passed through the courtyard here [in Buckingham Palace] at seven o'clock this morning. We stood on the balcony to see them. . . and an immense crowd collected to see these fine men, and cheering them immensely as they with difficulty marched along. They formed line [sic], presented arms, and then cheered us very heartily, and went off cheering. It was a touching and beautiful sight."[25] Stepping out from the shadow side of her life, as she referred to pregnancy and childbirth, she renewed her public personae as monarch of the nation, and in the process, recovered some of the power she had informally ceded to her husband. For as both Victoria and Albert recognized, the government and the British public had declared that the prince might advise the queen, but he would not govern in her stead.

The wartime queen seized upon the correction to be more assertive in family matters as well, a turn of events that introduced a good deal of coolness into the emotional and sexual life of the couple. Following Victoria's ninth delivery, doctors warned her and Albert that she should have no more children. Albert agreed with alacrity, warming quickly to the idea of a chaste marriage. As we have seen, Victoria did not share his enthusiasm for discontinuing sex, and she was more than willing to pay the price of additional pregnancies in order to keep her erotic life fulfilled. Gradually, however, she grew more and more resigned to chastity and began also to see Albert in something of a different light. Perhaps not coincidentally, this lessening of intense feeling for her husband took place at the same time she became increasingly involved with a man who would come to play an outsized—and to many, scandalous—role later in her life, John Brown, a ghillie on her estate at Balmoral. As a servant, Brown attended the queen on her visits to the Scottish castle the family had built, and as Albert seemed to slip a bit further from her life, Brown appears to have slipped in in his place. In one letter to Vicky, for example, Victoria wrote of how much she hated the life at Balmoral. A short time later, her letter told of a far cheerier state of affairs. "I and the girls lunched while Papa was after the stag—and good J. Brown was so attentive to us and so careful," she related to Vicky. "He is now my special servant, and there can't be a nicer, better or handier one . . . Brown has had everything to do for me indeed had charge of me on all, on all these expeditions, and therefore I settled that he should be specially appointed to attend on me (without any other title) and have a full dress suit. . . . Altogether I feel so sad—at the bitter thought of going from this blessed place—leaving these hills—this enchanting life of liberty—these dear people—and returning home to tame, dull, formal England and the prison life at Windsor."[26] It may be that Brown's attention to the queen and Albert's standoffishness account for the dramatic shift in her feelings about Balmoral and Windsor.

By late 1858 and 1859, Victoria's letters to her oldest daughter, Vicky, reveal the beginnings of a lukewarm feeling toward her husband. As she wrote in February 1861 about Albert having suffered from toothache, "dear Papa never allows he is any better or will try to get over it, but makes such a miserable face that people always think he's very ill. . . . His nervous system is easily excited and irritated, and he's so completely overpowered by everything."[27] Victoria's disenchantment with her husband in the last years of their marriage might well have produced real difficulties for the royal couple in the future, but the death of Albert at the end of 1861 made it possible for her to idealize him and their relationship till the end of her life. One wonders whether her endless, obsessive grief for Albert was not partly a product of the guilt she felt for having held less than positive feelings for him in the years before he died.

Despite the ups and downs of the relationship between Victoria and Albert, the royal couple presented to the British public the image of perfect domestic bliss. The innocence and modesty of the young queen, her marriage to Albert, the births of her numerous children, and her inconsolable grief upon her husband's death—these signaled to Britons of every class that the royal family was above all a family, embodying the characteristics of evangelicalism and what would come to be called bourgeois morality rather than those of a promiscuous aristocracy. The transformation of the monarchy from a debauched and profligate institution to one that exemplified and upheld the values of the middle classes in Britain ensured its survival at a time when crowns across the continent were being tossed into the gutter like trash.

CHAPTER 3

| CO-RULERS, 1842–1861: |
CHANGING IDEOLOGIES
OF GENDER AND RACE

VICTORIA AND ALBERT REIGNED AS CO-RULERS for two decades until his death at the end of 1861. During that time a number of challenges to the existing social and political order emerged, and Britain's relationship with its imperial holdings took on a different coloration. Some of these challenges brought about significant changes in the way Britons thought about gender and empire.

Victoria once famously declared, "we women, if we are to be good women, feminine and amiable and domestic, are not fitted to reign."[1] Her assertion reflected the broadly accepted assumptions of separate sphere ideology. But there existed in Britain a small cadre of people who contested these assumptions, who pointed out that although marriage and the family were firmly based on ideals of romantic love, companionship, and a spiritual equality between men and women, the legal, economic, and social position of women had yet to affirm that fact. For under the law of coverture, married women had no rights or existence apart from their husbands. The popular aphorism "my wife and I are one and I am he" described a situation in which a married woman had no legal rights to her property, her earnings, her freedom of movement, her conscience, her body, or her children; all resided in her husband. Throughout the nineteenth century, women and their male allies challenged these holdovers of aristocratic patriarchal society, insisting that rather than protecting women in the domestic sphere of home and family, these legal disabilities exposed them to the brutalities of the world at large. The contradictions of separate sphere ideology opened up space within which women could contest their positions of powerlessness, often utilizing the very language of women's special qualities to make their case for fundamental legal and political reform. Victoria vehemently opposed the efforts put forward by feminists, exposing the contradictions of a regnant queen in a system organized by separate sphere ideology. The women's movement, she railed, irritated her to the point that "she could not contain herself," and she was "most anxious to enlist every one who can speak or write to join in checking this mad, wicked folly of 'Women's Rights,' with all its attendant horrors, on which her poor feeble sex is bent, forgetting every sense of womanly feeling and propriety." Women involved in this monstrous campaign "ought to get a good whipping," she declared, for their search for equality with men rendered them "the most hateful, heathen and disgusting of beings" whose efforts would leave them without the protection of men, in which case they would perish.[2] In her condemnation she was not alone, but the women's movement nevertheless continued its steady, if slow, progress over the course of the nineteenth century.

The first challenge to property in women occurred in the 1830s, when Caroline Norton sued for control over her children after her husband absconded with them. The Custody Act of 1839 gave women custody of their children under the age of seven in cases of divorce or separation. Thereafter, the husband resumed control, though visitation rights were secured for his wife. The act modified but did not overturn paternal control, for any father had complete authority over his children, determining their domicile, the extent and location of their schooling, their religion, and their guardianship, but it served to crack the legal edifice within which women existed as chattel, as the property of husbands or fathers.

Caroline Norton brought her action in order to alleviate her own personal sufferings, not out of any feminist intention. As she wrote to Queen Victoria in 1855, she wholeheartedly embraced the belief that "the natural position of woman is inferiority to man. That is a thing of God's appointing, not of man's devising. I believe it sincerely, as part of my religion. I never pretended to the wild and ridiculous doctrine of equality."[3] But her actions had a profound impact on the lives of women, paving the way for other reforms that dramatically opened up possibilities for women that simply did not exist before. Her husband, George Norton, from whom she was separated, had borrowed money against her marriage settlement and refused to pay the debts he had incurred on her behalf. In 1853, one of her creditors, with her permission, sued her husband for payment of her debts. Norton recounted the events of the trial in *English Laws for Women*, in which she laid out the disabilities women suffered under common law and especially that of the doctrine of coverture. Its publication made clear in vivid terms the kinds of injustices women suffered under the law, and it powerfully influenced subsequent campaigns to reform it. As we will see in Chapter 5, those efforts resulted in women being able to own their own property and earnings by means of the passage of the Married Women's Property Acts of 1870, 1882, and 1893.

The early supporters of women's rights frequently characterized women's position in society as analogous to slavery; many of them, in fact, had come to their feminist positions after having served at length in the antislavery campaign. Without the means to become financially independent of men, women would forever be locked into the same situation of vulnerability to abuse from men as African slaves experienced at the hands of their masters. For women such as Bessie Raynor Parkes and Barbara Leigh Smith Bodichon, women's inability to find respectable work by which they might support themselves, and, indeed, to actually end up owning for themselves any wages they might earn, rendered them unable to leave abusive or potentially abusive situations.

Bodichon's *A Brief Summary in Plain Language of the Most Important Laws Concerning Women*, published in 1854, laid out in a systematic fashion the legal situation that condemned women to a position of chattel of men. The solution to these problems lay in increasing educational and employment possibilities for women and obtaining the passage of bills that gave married women the right to own property and retain their earnings, just as femes sole might currently do. To this end, these "ladies of Langham Place," as they came to be called after the location of their office in London, founded the *English Woman's Journal* in 1858. In its pages, contributors publicized the cause of women throughout Britain, raising issues of concern for women such as property rights and divorce laws.

Langham Place also provided space for the Society for Promoting the Employment of Women, founded by Jessie Boucherett in 1859 to provide a kind of clearing house of employment opportunities for mostly middle-class women without means of support outside the overcrowded, low-paying, and humiliating profession of governessing, which was currently the only work they might obtain without compromising their class position. The Society argued that middle-class parents must recognize that their daughters might not be able to marry, given the redundancy of women relative to men, and must be educated for work beyond governessing or teaching. They recognized that for women to become economically independent of men they must break down the barriers that kept them from being educated in sound educational institutions for work that was remunerative. Queen's College had been founded in 1848 and began to grant degrees to women. In the 1850s, Mary Frances Buss and Dorothea Beale had opened the North of London Collegiate School for Ladies and Cheltenham Ladies' College, respectively, so that single middle-class women might qualify for employment that would provide an income to support them.

Women obtained some amelioration even from the law that most symbolized their status as property—that of divorce, and here again Caroline Norton played a crucial role. Until 1857, divorce in England could be obtained only by act of parliament and was available only to the wealthy elite. The Matrimonial Causes Act of 1857 created a court for divorce and established grounds for the procedure. Men could divorce their wives, as before, on the basis of adultery alone; women, however, had to prove their husbands' adultery *and* cruelty, desertion, incest, rape, sodomy, or bestiality. The Royal Commission on Divorce, reporting in 1850, had recommended that adultery was much more serious on the part of the wife than of the husband. The Matrimonial Causes Act, however much it incorporated a double standard of behavior for men and women in England and Wales (in Scotland, a single standard of infidelity for either spouse prevailed, and in Ireland, adherence to Catholic doctrines prohibiting divorce by the vast majority of the population rendered laws made in Westminster moot), did allow divorce for women. Many of the protective clauses of the act—which, for example, gave separated women the rights to own and inherit property, to enter into contracts and to sue or be sued, and to receive monetary support decided upon by a court and not by an aggrieved husband—were influenced by Norton's *A Letter to the Queen on Lord Cranworth's Marriage and Divorce Bill*, published in 1855.

The antislavery campaign had broad-based and long-lasting ramifications beyond that of helping to spur the rise of a women's movement. The situation of slaves appeared to many people to resemble that of white women at the hands of white men and helped to galvanize large numbers of mostly middle-class British women to demand their own freedoms and rights. More immediately, the abolition of slavery led Britons to draw firmer lines between black and white peoples so that hierarchical relations of power could be sustained in the absence of legal differentiations based on race. Moreover, the end of slavery helped to further the imperial project. Once Britons could no longer be regarded as responsible for slavery in their own territories, blame for the continuation of the institution could be shifted onto others, particularly Americans, and, more and more, onto Africans themselves, who, moralists asserted, relied on the slave trade to sustain their economies. In 1841, combining missionary zeal with political economy, Thomas Fowell Buxton, with the strong support of Prince Albert and the approval and financial backing of the British government, launched an expedition to the Niger in West Africa to end slavery and establish proper commercial undertakings there. As depicted by Buxton's campaign literature and publicity, Africa was a place of darkness and barbarism. "Bound in the chains of the grossest ignorance," he wrote, its people fell "prey to the most savage superstition." Slavery, torture, butchery, human sacrifices, cannibalism, dismemberment, infanticide—these practices could be ended and African peoples redeemed by showing Africans alternative methods of using their material resources, by establishing commercial ventures in agriculture and trade in commodities, and by setting up schools and missions through which to educate Africans in European and Christian ways. Harriet Martineau's protagonist in *Dawn Island*, a novel written in 1845 on behalf of the campaign to repeal the Corn Laws in Britain and establish free trade throughout the empire, expressed the confidence of many influential Britons about the possibility of civilizing barbaric peoples by preaching to them the gospel of Christ and laissez-faire. "It warmed my heart and filled my head," Buxton declared, "to see how these children of nature were clearly destined to be carried on some way towards becoming men and Christians by my bringing Commerce to their shores."[4]

The Niger expedition failed spectacularly. Of the 150 white Britons who set out to stamp out slavery at its source in the hinterlands of West Africa, forty-four died of malaria. Most of the remaining Britons, themselves ill with fever, withdrew from a model farm they had set up with 150 Africans from the coast. When Britons returned the next year to bring relief to the settlers, they found the farm in disarray and fields planted with cotton and maize barren. Warfare between various ethnic groups in the area had produced refugees looking to escape the bloodshed; these had been put to work by the settlers, who, it was reported, would do no work themselves. "I found them indolent and lazy," reported Lieutenant William Webb, the head of the relief expedition, "not one willing or even disposed to manual labour, but ready enough to exercise authority over the negroes they hired." Reports of settlers molesting the refugee women circulated, as did a story about the settlers using whips "apparently for the purpose of urging the natives to greater exertion." What had begun as a great moral undertaking to bring salvation and enlightenment to the savage peoples of Africa had turned into a debacle. Not only had the trade in slaves not been abolished, but the settlers charged with establishing alternative forms of commerce had apparently resorted to slavery themselves. As *The Times* put it scathingly upon hearing the accounts of Webb and others, "the Niger Anti-Slavery Expedition has . . . planted a *very* 'model' of the most cruel and iniquitous SLAVERY, and that in a spot where such, as at least such systematic scourge-bearing slavery, was probably unknown before."[5]

The disaster of the Niger Expedition combined with other developments to help transform British racial thought after 1850. Charles Dickens sounded one of the first blasts against the prevailing liberal view that all races were equal in capacity and could be raised up to European levels in his excoriation of the anti-slavery campaigners in an 1848 article entitled "The Niger Expedition." "Between the civilized European and the barbarous African," he insisted, "there is a great gulf set. . . . To change the customs even of civilized . . . men . . . is . . . a most difficult and slow proceeding; but to do this by ignorant and savage races, is a work which, like the progressive changes of the globe itself, requires a stretch of years that dazzles in the looking at." Only fools could expect to "railroad" savages into Christianity and civilization, he asserted, and they should not waste their efforts in a land as dark and benighted as Africa.[6] Thomas Carlyle, a celebrated intellectual and man of letters, followed suit the next year, when he denounced the abolition of slavery as a ruinous failure for the economies of the West Indies and declared blacks an inferior race of peoples fit only for the yoke of compulsory labor. During the 1840s, sugar exports from the West Indies to Britain dropped as competition from other sugar cane producers and from the production of sugar beets in Europe increased. In 1846, when parliament repealed the Corn Laws, removing protective tariffs on grain entering Britain, and ushering in the era of free trade, planters in Jamaica feared for their economic livelihood. They turned to Carlyle to plead their cause before the British public. His "Occasional Discourse on the Nigger Question," published in *Fraser's Magazine* in 1849, established many of the basic elements that would characterize British racial thinking in the years after 1850.

In "The Nigger Question,"[7] Carlyle railed against the "troublous condition" of Jamaica caused by the abolition of slavery and called for a version of it to be reintroduced in order to save black and white Jamaicans alike from destitution and degradation. Blacks would not work, he asserted, repeating the allegations of Jamaican planters who saw in blacks' preference to cultivate their own plots to sell crops at market rather than work on plantations for low wages a manifestation of their "laziness," a refusal to work. He depicted them "sitting yonder with their beautiful muzzles up to the ears in pumpkins," by which he meant melons or tropical fruit like papaya or mango, "imbibing sweet pulps and juices; the grinder and incisor teeth ready for ever new work, and the pumpkins cheap as grass in those rich climates: while the sugar-crops rot around them uncut, because labour cannot be hired, so cheap are the pumpkins." Compel them to work, Carlyle exhorted his audience, for no man had the right "to eat pumpkin" who would not labor on the plantations. "If Quashee," as Carlyle styled Jamaican blacks derisively, "will not honestly aid in bringing-out those sugars, cinnamons and nobler products of the West-Indian Islands, for the benefit of all mankind, then I say neither will the Powers permit Quashee to continue growing pumpkins there for his own lazy benefit; but will shear him out, . . . perhaps in a terrible manner." The gods had ordained that "spices and valuable products be grown in their West Indies," Carlyle explained; even more, "they wish, that manful industrious men occupy their West Indies, not indolent two-legged cattle." Compel them to work with the whip, if need be, he continued, for it was unlikely that Quashee would be induced to labor as white men had been by the promise of delayed gratifications. "Quashee, if he will not help in bringing-out the spices, will get himself made a slave again . . ., and with beneficent whip, since other methods avail not, will be compelled to work."

Carlyle saw in slavery, or its preferred alternative, a system of "servants hired for life," the proper and divinely ordered relationship of "wise men" to foolish others, of the industrious to the "lazy," of the "strong to the weak; of the great and noble-minded to the small and mean!" He applied his condemnations to all men who would not work, but coded such people as "black." "They also," he observed of "rich white men," "have long sat Negro-like up to the ears in pumpkin." Negroes, for Carlyle, served as the model for all manner of indolence, insolence, corruption, and savagery, and their very inferiority demanded that they serve whites. "Decidedly you have to be servants to those that are born *wiser* than you, that are born lords of you; servants to the Whites, if they *are* (as what mortal can doubt they are?) born wiser than you."

Carlyle's "Nigger Question" represented blacks in feminine terms, as entities with feminine qualities in need of manly mastery. "I decidedly like poor Quashee," he wrote in the 1853 edition, "and find him a pretty kind of man. . . . a merry-hearted, grinning, dancing, singing, affectionate kind of creature, with a great deal of melody and amenability in his composition." For Carlyle, in fact, the great problem was not poor Quashee at all, but the effeminate, soft evangelical philanthropists and liberal political economists who had emancipated him in the first place. "Windy sentimentalists," he called them, lumping them in with "women and children and stump-orators" who weep over trifles like slavery, while "serious men who have work to do in this Universe" recognized that wise men, superior men must rule over others, over the inferior if order and governance were to prevail. "Well, *except* by Mastership and Servantship, there is no conceivable deliverance from Tyranny and Slavery," he declared with exasperation. In his formulations, which cannot be considered mainstream at the time they were written, but did become so in the second half of the nineteenth century, the concept of manliness did not embrace abolitionism and liberal understandings of human equality across lines of race. Rather, people who held such positions demonstrated effeminate qualities, as did the objects of their concerns, slaves and other people of color, and their projects would serve only to corrupt the proper ordering of British society. The wedding of evangelical philanthropists and political economists in the cause of "Black Emancipation, or the like," Carlyle promised, invoking gendered and perverse sexual imagery, "will give birth to progenies and prodigies; dark extensive moon-calves, unnamable abortions, wide-coiled monstrosities, such as the world has not seen hitherto!"[8]

Victoria and Albert despised this kind of racial hatred. The queen often expressed "her very strong feeling (and she has few stronger) that the natives and coloured races should be treated with every kindness and affection, as brothers, not—as, alas! Englishmen too often do—as totally different to ourselves, fit only to be crushed and shot down!" The royal couple instilled their sentiments in the Prince of Wales, who himself asserted, "Because a man has a black face and a different religion from our own, there is no reason why he should be treated as a brute." British society had shared these beliefs—or at least the profession of them—in the first half of the nineteenth century. Even when that changed in later years, members of the royal family maintained their respect for racial and religious diversity, and made their views known. As Victoria was to say, "*all* her Colonial Governors should *know* her feelings on this *subject* of the *native races*."[9]

Victoria's goddaughter, Sarah Forbes Bonetta, 1862.

In 1850, Victoria and Albert brought into their domestic circle as goddaughter a seven-year-old Yoruba girl who had been captured by Dahomean slavers. The king of Dahomey had been persuaded by the captain of an antislavery squadron vessel, Commander Frederick Forbes, to give the captive girl to Queen Victoria as "a present from the King of the Blacks to the Queen of the Whites."[10] Commander Forbes had her baptized and named her Sarah Bonetta Forbes (Bonetta being the name of his ship), and brought her back to England to meet the royal family at Windsor Castle.

She visited regularly over the next year, but unaccustomed to the chilly and smoggy London climate, she fell ill with a cough. Forbes had died by then, and the decision was made to return Sarah to West Africa, where she would be educated by

missionaries in Freetown, Sierra Leone. Victoria paid for her education and followed her career closely through missionaries
who returned home on leave. When Samuel Crowder, the Yoruba
missionary who had accompanied the Niger Expedition and who
would become the first black bishop in West Africa, visited Prince
Albert in 1851 to report on antislavery activities, Queen Victoria
entered the room and joined the free-flowing conversation about
the state of the slave trade. Crowther did not know it was her—
"a lady came in," he recalled, "simply dressed"[11]—until Albert
asked Her Majesty to bring over a candle. She set him at his ease
and then inquired after her goddaughter.

Sarah Forbes returned to London to visit the queen and her
family fairly regularly. She attended the wedding of the queen's
oldest daughter, the Princess Royal Victoria, in 1862 and received
the queen's permission to marry that same year. She named her
own daughter after the queen, who became the child's god-
mother. Sarah and the young Victoria visited the queen in 1867,
but Sarah would not be able to return to England again, owing to
ill health. She died in 1880 at the age of thirty-seven, but the
queen continued to look after the young Victoria, seeing to her
education at Cheltenham Ladies' College and providing her with
an annuity. As one historian has pointed out, Queen Victoria extended her position as mother to the nation to include the empire
as well, sometimes literally.[12]

Thomas Carlyle linked what he saw as the parlous state of
Jamaica to the situation in Ireland, from which he had just returned when he first wrote "The Nigger Question." He accused
liberal politicians of having produced there what he feared
would occur in Jamaica if blacks were not forced to work, "a *Black
Ireland*; 'free' indeed, but an Ireland, and Black!" Their free trade
policies, in conjunction with Irish laziness, he charged, referring
in racial and sexual terms to the millions of people suffering
from famine, had given rise to not a white but to a "sallow Ireland,
sluttishly starving from age to age on its act-of-parliament 'freedom.'" The Irish, like blacks in Jamaica, he declared in a letter to

A SCENE IN FAMINE. — A WIDOW AND CHILDREN OF THE O'CONNELL ESTATES ON THEIR WAY TO BEG POTATOES.

Irish Potato Famine, 1846.

Ralph Waldo Emerson, would "have to learn that man does need government, and that an able-bodied starving beggar is and remains . . . a SLAVE destitute of a MASTER."[13]

In 1845, Ireland suffered a potato blight, which worsened in 1846 and again in 1847 and 1848. By the 1840s, the potato had become the staple crop for millions of Irish peasants, and when it failed those peasants had very little else to turn to. In the years 1845 to 1851, the country lost some 2.25 million people, perhaps half of them to death by starvation or disease, the other half to emigration to England, Australia and New Zealand, Canada, and the United States. Robert Peel, Tory prime minister, responded robustly to the crisis in 1845, purchasing 20,000 tons of Indian corn and meal from the United States and exporting it to Ireland. Though initially difficult to digest and causing pretty severe gastric problems, both because it had not been ground fine enough and because Irish stomachs were unused to it, the Indian corn soon proved sufficient to feed most of the Irish who needed it. Peel also pushed through the government the repeal of the Corn Laws, which had artificially raised prices on imported grains so that English landlords could sell their crops at good prices. This step ultimately cost Peel the leadership of his party, and the party its power, but he was determined to see the repeal through. He enjoyed the support of Victoria and Albert, as well as their admiration for his bravery in advocating repeal. The queen wrote to her uncle Leopold of her *"extreme* admiration of our worthy Peel, who shows himself a man of unbounded *loyalty, courage,* patriotism, and *high-mindedness.* . . . I have never seen him so excited or so determined, and *such* a good cause must succeed."[14] Albert showed his support for the measure by sitting in the gallery of the House of Commons during the debate over repealing the Corn Laws, an act that backfired when a prominent Tory rebuked him for showing favoritism to the prime minister.

The action of Peel's government in 1845 and 1846 prevented disaster. But when the harvest failed again in 1846, the new Whig government fell far short of what was needed to relieve the hunger of so vast a population. Imbued with the ideology of laissez-faire, which preached nonintervention by the government in the workings of the economy, the Whig minister in charge of the situation, Charles Trevelyan, refused to ban the exportation of grain from Ireland. This led to increased deprivation and then starvation, which in turn made the population vulnerable to infectious diseases. The government tried to address the problem by putting Irish peasants to work on public works projects, by establishing soup kitchens, and then by increasing the eligibility for assistance under the poor laws by making it possible for people not entering the poor house to receive aid. This last effort, however, included a provision put forward by a large landholding Irish MP that no one could receive relief without surrendering their land holdings to their landlords. This meant, in effect, that Irish peasants either lost access to the land or that they starved because they would not give up their land. This provision proved to be the strongest evidence to later Irish nationalists that the British had intentionally starved the Irish, committing, in essence, genocide.

This was not the case, but it was not hard to believe the charge, given the lack of information about what the government was doing and the unbelievably callous statements in the press regarding the famine. Victoria expressed her distress over the Irish situation in her journal and in speeches read to parliament, and gave generously from her own funds to the private relief efforts mobilized by British and American philanthropists. She headed the patron list of the fund created by London bankers and merchants and attended benefit performances on behalf of relief efforts. She lent her name to requests for aid in churches, and she did what she could to alleviate the disaster unfolding across the Irish Sea. It was not much, however, for death rates began to skyrocket, and for the next five years, famine and disease stalked the land.

While Irish liberals and nationalists attributed the disaster of the Great Famine to English land tenure policies and the existence of an absentee Anglo-Irish landowning class, English and Scottish liberals in parliament and conservatives in and out of government believed the famine to have come about as a consequence of Irish character and morality. As *The Times* asserted in 1843 before the famine broke out, "Ireland and the Irish have, in a great measure themselves to thank for their poverty and want of capital. . . . It is by industry, toil, perseverance, economy, prudence, by self-denial, and self-dependence, that a state becomes mighty and its people happy." The English and northern Irish Protestants had demonstrated such national traits, and the Irish Catholics, by contrast, suffered from the lack of them. They would not work, the paper added in 1845. "Of all the Celtic tribes, famous everywhere for their indolence and fickleness as the Celts everywhere are," intoned *Fraser's Magazine* in 1847, "the Irish are admitted to be the most idle and most fickle." The satiric magazine *Punch* reported them to be the laziest and dirtiest people in the world, descended from "generations of beggars. You can trace the descent in their blighted, stunted forms—in their brassy, cunning, brutalized features."[15]

The Irish became the "white negroes" of Europe. Like Africans, black Jamaicans, and people of color throughout the world, the Irish—when acting peaceably and not making demands for repeal of the Act of Union of 1800 and the establishment of their own legislature, or setting the countryside ablaze in agrarian riots protesting lack of land security and food—were depicted in somewhat benign but decidedly unmanly terms. They were "a people of acute sensibilities and lively passions," asserted *The Times* in 1843 in terms usually applied to women, "more quick in feeling wrongs than rational in explaining or temperate in addressing them—as easily roused into outrage by supposed oppression as subdued into docility by felicitous kindness." Like women, they were impulsive, inconsistent, contradictory, passionate, and prone to exaggeration, and until they demonstrated a manly kind of behavior, they would be ruled as if they were women, dependent and in need of a controlling hand.[16]

When not behaving as the English wished, as in the repeal campaign and during agrarian outrages, the Irish became savage, with all the sexual overtones implied therein, in British representations of them. Benjamin Disraeli, future prime minister of Britain, accused Daniel O'Connell, the leader of the repeal movement, of behaving disreputably, implying a sexual immorality and an unmanliness that no proper Englishman would demonstrate. His "public life and private life are equally profligate," charged Disraeli; "he has committed every crime that does not require courage." Irish Protestants claimed that Catholic priests urged their parishioners to fall upon their Protestant neighbors with bestial fury. "From the altar, inflamed by bigotry and delighting in blood, rush out the savage populace," declared one pamphlet, "to seize upon the victim, and to consign to destruction his property, his family, his home, and his life." George Cruikshank's 1845 illustration of the "Murder of George Crawford and his Granddaughter," recalling the Irish revolt during the Napoleonic wars, shows Irish peasants with brutish, apelike faces running pikes through the two victims and a dog. Crawford's granddaughter has gone to his aid, pleading for them to stop, just as one rebel pierces her breast with his weapon. People like this, Britons believed, brought upon themselves the very ills they protested—poverty and famine, unemployment and landlessness, and coercive legislation from an administration firm in its resolve to bring order to an uncivilized nation. "When Ireland acts according to the principles of civilised man," announced *The Times* in 1846, "then she can be ruled by the laws of civilised man."[17] Until that time, harsh British rule would remain. British politicians, journalists, satirists, novelists, and clergy conjured up a picture of a manly Britain ruling over a feminized, effeminate Ireland.

The paradox of such a depiction became obvious when, in 1849, Queen Victoria made her first visit to her Irish subjects. She did so following a series of violent but ineffectual outbreaks across the country by members of Young Ireland, a movement attempting to capitalize on the revolutions that were breaking out across the continent in 1848. Victoria had feared as late as October 1848 that the loyalty of Ireland was dubious, describing a country "quivering in our grasp, and ready to throw off her allegiance at any moment."[18] The May 1849 attempt by an unemployed Irishman from County Limerick to assassinate the queen only confirmed her and her ministers in their decision that a royal tour of Ireland was overdue.

The visit proved successful. Crowds throughout the country turned out enthusiastically to welcome the royal couple, and in Dublin the people vividly made known their affection for the queen. She was struck by the poverty she saw, confiding to her journal that "the raggedness of the people is beyond belief, man & boy having really hardly any covering, for they never mend anything"; yet she was impressed that even the poorest women had "such beautiful black eyes and hair and such fine colours and teeth." She brought up the dreadful experience of the famine, telling Dubliners that "I gladly share with you the hope that the heavy visitation with which Providence has recently visited large number of people in this country is passing away. I have felt deeply for their sufferings, and it will be a source of heartfelt satisfaction to me if I am permitted to witness the future and lasting prosperity of this portion of the United Kingdom."[19]

Immediately following her return from Ireland, Victoria created Bertie, the seven-year-old heir to the throne, the Earl of Dublin. A year later, she christened her third son Arthur William Patrick Albert, perhaps in response to a woman who had called out to her in Ireland the previous year, "Ah, Queen dear, make one of them Prince Patrick and Ireland will die for you."[20] The queen and Albert made two more trips to Ireland—in 1853 and 1861—but following the prince's death at the end of 1861, Victoria let the bonds she had created with the Irish people fray, a circumstance that would bode ill for Anglo-Irish relations over the next half century.

Liberal understandings of racial differences and racial inequality as circumstantial and removable had come under attack, as we have seen, by the end of the 1840s as the voices of men like Thomas Carlyle and Charles Dickens began to make themselves heard in an increasingly louder tones. Still, it was not until 1857, with the outbreak of the Indian Mutiny, as the British called it, that the liberal views of men like John Stuart Mill were drowned out by far more conservative assertions of the irremediable, biological nature of racial differences and inequalities. The Indian rebellion, followed by the terror campaign of the Irish Fenians and by the revolt of black Jamaicans in 1865, which we will treat in the next chapter, led the vast majority of Britons to embrace the "scientific" racial views propagated by social Darwinism after 1860 that located racial difference in evolutionary stages and rendered racial inequalities a matter of evolutionary, biological development. Grounded in nature, most Britons believed, inequalities could not be redressed by social or political means.

The rebellion broke out in May 1857, when Indian sepoys of the Bengal army rose up against their British officers and marched to Delhi, where they proclaimed the descendant of the last Mogul

Indian Mutiny, 1857.

ruler, Bahadur Shah, emperor of Hindustan. From Delhi, the revolt spread across much of northern India, attracting alienated groups from all parts of society. For more than a year, Hindus and Muslims, merchants and landowners, princes and peasants fought against and in many cases removed local British authorities till it seemed that the British might be ousted altogether. They were not, but it took at least fourteen months before the army that had remained loyal to Britain, made up predominately of the "manly" warrior race of Sikhs, was able to reestablish control in large parts of Oudh and the Punjab and reassert their authority and rule over the subcontinent as a whole.

The mutiny destroyed Britons' confidence in their liberal view of empire. They had understood their mission in India and elsewhere to be that of educating and Christianizing the indigenous population to the point where they could expect someday, even if that day were long off, to govern themselves. They had believed they were bringing progress and improvement to people who had fallen under the sway of "oriental despots" but who, because they were born rational men and with exposure to liberal reforms, education, free trade, and Christianity, could learn the ways of self-government. Now, the *Economist* declared in a classic statement of conservative versus liberal views of empire in September 1857, Britons had to decide "whether in future India is to be governed *as a Colony or as a Conquest*; whether we are to rule our Asiatic subjects with strict and generous justice, wisely and beneficently, as their natural and indefeasible superiors, by virtue of our higher civilization, our purer religion, our sterner energies . . . or whether we are to regard the Hindoos and Mahomedans as our equal fellow citizens, fit to be entrusted with the functions of self-government, ripe (or to be ripened) for British institutions, likely to appreciate the blessings of our rule, and, therefore, to be gradually prepared, as our own working classes are preparing, for a full participation in the privileges of representative assemblies, trial by jury, and all the other palladia of English liberty."[21] The answer was clear. If previously loyal sepoys, trained in the military discipline of the British army, proved so ungrateful for the tutelage of their British masters as to betray them at the first opportunity, how could other, less developed, natives be expected to respond? In Oudh, especially, which the British annexed in 1856, dislodging the nawab and the local aristocracy and bestowing property rights upon the peasantry, the British expected the peasantry to side with them against the rebels. Instead, they followed their ruler and nobles in revolt, a clear sign of their irrationality and inability to pursue their own interests. Just how possible would it be for people who demonstrated so incomplete an appreciation for their own interests that they would rise against those who sought to act for them in their own interests to rule themselves? So demonstrably irrational were the actions of the Indian people that they could not be perceived any longer to be like Britons at heart and be expected to respond to efforts to educate and civilize them.

From this moment on, Britons would see their role in India as one of conquest rather than civilization and regard Indians not as human beings potentially like themselves but as wholly and utterly different who would need British rule if order were to be established and kept. In 1858, with the Government of India Act, the government abolished the East India Company, which had operated in a quasi-contractual fashion under the local rulers of Indian states, and placed two-thirds of the land of the subcontinent under the authority of the queen. The remaining one-third of the country stayed in the hands of Indian princes, maharajas, and maharanis who retained their independence and the freedom to determine the domestic policies of their states. In the royal proclamation that ended the rule of India by the East India Company and made it a crown colony to be ruled directly from London, Victoria and Albert insisted on language that softened the severity of crown rule. The proclamation "cannot possibly remain in its present shape," Albert protested. They strenuously objected to a clause that asserted the queen's power to "undermine native religions and customs," calling instead for a document that would "breathe feelings of generosity, benevolence and religious toleration." The proclamation, Victoria insisted, should "draw a veil over the sad and bloody past" and make clear that the solace she derived from her own religion "will preclude her from an attempt to interfere with the native religions."[22] They prevailed, though such feelings did not translate into equivalent actions on the ground in India.

The mutiny led a significant portion of the British public to argue that Indians were not just unlike themselves but were inhuman, cruel savages. Throughout the rebellion and long after, tales of the most horrible atrocities committed by Indian men against the British, and most especially against British women, circulated throughout India and the home country. Victoria wrote to Lady Canning, wife of India's viceroy, to ask if they could "ascertain how far these are true." She noted that even British soldiers in times of war might commit murder against women and children; what she wished to know was "whether there is any reliable evidence of eyewitnesses—of horrors, like people having to eat their children's flesh—and other unspeakable and dreadful atrocities which I could not write?"[23] She doubted them, and was right to do so, as these stories could not be verified, and in fact were later debunked by British officials. Nevertheless, accounts of rape, torture, mutilation, and murder of "our countrywomen" continued to circulate as truth. They electrified the British public, searing the British imagination with pictures of scalped and dismembered white women, infants cut from their mothers' wombs, children burned alive, and women crucified. In private letters home, newspapers in Bombay and London, histories of the mutiny, and in subsequent novels right up through the 1960s and 1970s, the rape of English women served as the indelible sign of Indian savagery. Colonial insurrection, rebellion against imperial rule, took on not the dimensions of a political act carried out by oppressed people seeking to overthrow foreign domination but of a sexual crime committed against an English woman, indeed against all of British womanhood.

In story after story, British women and girls were stripped of their clothes, sexually molested, and thrown to the masses for further abuse. One clergyman claimed in a letter to *The Times* that he witnessed Indians taking "48 females, most of them girls of from 10 to 14, many delicately nurtured ladies,—violated them and kept for the base purposes of the heads of the insurrection for a whole week. At the end of that time they made them strip themselves, and gave them up to the lowest of the people to abuse in broad daylight in the street of Delhi. They then commenced the work of torturing them to death, cutting off their breasts, fingers, and noses, and leaving them to die. One lady was three days dying." Reports of a massacre of British hostages at Cawnpore by a rebel leader, Nana Sahib, took on immense proportions as a myth of mass rape and torture grew up around the execution of 200 British women and children by Nana Sahib's retreating forces. The rebels threw the women's bodies into a well in order to conceal them. Subsequent official investigations found no evidence of rape or torture, but the site of the massacre, the Bibighar, became a shrine to desecrated womanhood for the British soldiers marching through. They passed stories of violated women along to their fellow soldiers and left messages written in blood on the walls of the Bibighar that purported to be from the "Mutiny ladies" demanding that their hideous treatment at the hands of Nana Sahib be avenged. Rebels, and Nana Sahib in particular, took on the persona of sexually sadistic monsters in novels about the mutiny.[24] George Trevelyan's history of the mutiny, *Cawnpore*, published in 1865, attributed its outbreak to "the ambition of the soldiery. . . . Chafing under restraint, they panted to indulge themselves in unbridled rapine and licence." In James Grant's *First Love and Last Love: A Tale of the Indian Mutiny*, published in 1868 after the atrocity stories had been discredited by British officials investigating them, "women were outraged again and again, ere they were slaughtered, riddled with musket balls, or gashed by bayonets; and every indignity that the singularly fiend-ish invention of the Oriental mind could suggest, was offered to the dying and the dead." Grant charged that the sexual proclivi-ties of Indians, along with "religious fanaticism and Oriental cruelty," had caused the rebellion. "Had not the Nana Sahib at Cawnpore . . . slain the Christian women by the hundreds and flung them into a well, because not one of them would enter his zenana?" he demanded.[25]

Certainly British women and children, like those at Cawnpore, as well as British men, died at the hands of the rebels. But most of them died from shots fired in battle or from diseases they con-tracted during long sieges of their towns and stations, where lack of clean water, food, and medical supplies made them susceptible to cholera and dysentery. Such deaths, however, could not readily be mobilized to justify a ferocious British response to the revolt, in which British soldiers retaliated against the rebels by execut-ing whole villages, burning civilians and soldiers alive, and blow-ing Indians out of a cannon. Victoria was appalled by the reprisals against the Indian population and urged restraint. She regarded cries of revenge like those of an assistant commissioner in India that "all should be shot like dogs" as "too horrible and really quite shameful." Certainly those who had committed atrocities should be punished, and firmly, but she urged that only the "greatest kindness" should be extended to the "many kind and friendly natives" who had stayed loyal to the British. "They should know," she asserted, "that there is no hatred to a brown skin—none; but the greatest wish on the Queen's part to see them happy, contented and flourishing."[26]

The outrages committed by British soldiers against sepoys and Indian civilians were reported at the time and in later nineteenth- and twentieth-century historical accounts to have been the consequence of uncontrollable fury provoked by the rape and torture of British women and children by the sepoys. "Remember the Ladies! Remember the Babies!" they were reported as crying as they rode into battle seeking revenge from men who had degraded their women and desecrated their homes. George Lawrence's fictional character in *Maurice Dering* (1864) journeys to India to avenge the death of his fiancé. He explains that her "foul murder" incited him to previously unthinkable actions. "Has any one forgotten the evil Spring, when there swept over this country of ours a blast from the East—fatal to many households . . . chilling to many hearts . . . ? Have we forgotten how, with each successive mail, the wrath and the horror grew wilder; till the sluggish Anglo-Saxon nature became, as it were, possessed by a devil, and through the length and breadth of the land . . . there went up one awful cry for vengeance?" Urged by a minister to show mercy to his enemies, he refuses because they had no thought of mercy "when my innocent darling was given up to those unchained devils." "He gnashed his teeth as he spoke, and his moustache grew white and wet with foam."[27]

In accordance with a logic that saw in the status and treatment of women a measure of civilization, Indian men and men of color generally came, as a consequence of the mutiny, to be regarded as defilers of innocent British women, till the image of the rape and mutilation of white women by black men came to stand not merely for the mutiny itself but for the whole relationship of

Britain to its colonial subjects. And white men, Britons, having responded with fury at the outrages committed against their women, as the new imperial narrative had it, would see their mission as one of protecting innocent, chaste white women from black men and saving black women from black men as well. "We who live among the records and associations of chivalry," wrote Trevelyan, "still make it our pride to regard women as goddesses. The Hindoos, . . . the Mohammedans . . . cannot bring themselves to look upon them as better than playthings."[28]

A new model of British manliness began to emerge from the events and accounts surrounding the Indian rebellion. No longer exclusively the Christian man of reason, as embodied by the minister urging mercy upon the hero in *Maurice Dering*, but also a man of action, passion, and romance, the post-rebellion prototype of English manliness possessed a love of justice; he was slow to anger but capable when provoked of meting out a terrible, violent retribution against his foes. A man of body more than of mind now, as the notion of muscular Christianity promoted by Charles Kingsley suggests, he nevertheless continued to demonstrate his capacity to reason, one of the most important elements in distinguishing this newly aggressive Briton from the manly warrior tribes like the Sihks. With the infusion of scientific arguments about racial superiority and inferiority drawn from the evolutionary theories of Charles Darwin, the story of imperialism changed from one of liberal Christian gentlemen bringing free trade, civilization, and the tools of self-government to childlike, feminized peoples of lesser development to that of an aggressive, powerful, authoritarian, racially superior British nation conquering savage, sexualized, and feminized lands and establishing order over subhuman, animal-like "niggers" of a biologically inferior breed.

Starting in 1846, a very different kind of rule emerged in the white colonies of settlement ruled by Britain, though Victoria seems to have taken little interest in them. At that time, some 750,000 Britons and an equal number of French inhabited

Canada, the vast bulk of which remained unsettled by Europeans; perhaps 70,000 Europeans lived on twelve islands in the Caribbean; the five convict colonies established in Australia in the eighteenth century had grown into settlements with their own legislatures, and Sydney, the capital of New South Wales, enjoyed a population of 30,000 Britons; New Zealand had only recently been colonized by whites after the British government in 1840 signed a treaty with Maori chiefs that, in the name of Te Kuini Wikitoria (Queen Victoria), gave them "full, exclusive and undisputed possession of their lands and estates,"[29] a promise that would not be honored for long; and South Africa contained around 20,000 Britons and 40,000 Afrikaners or Boers, descendants of the Dutch who had settled on the Cape of Good Hope in the seventeenth century. These colonies of settlement differed wildly from one another, but ultimately all but some of those in the Caribbean would come to enjoy what came to be called "responsible government" in their relationship to their sovereign queen.

The solution of responsible government appealed to a variety of constituencies in both the white colonies and at home. Some Britons in the metropole, the experience of the American colonies still strong in their minds, believed that the white colonies should be let go before they proved to be a source of trouble. Evangelicals, on the other hand, doubted that white colonists could be counted on to treat indigenous peoples or descendants of African slaves with the respect they deserved; they insisted that rule from Britain was required to protect them from oppression. Political and military strategists saw in the white settlements the means by which to ensure their control of the oceans and feared that if they were let go, other powers would simply scoop them up to further their own ambitions. Colonial reformers such as Edward Gibbon Wakefield believed further colonization of the white territories would alleviate the social problems Britain faced as industrialization displaced thousands of people and hunger stalked the land. For the white settlers themselves, colonial rule had begun to rankle, and sometimes vociferous demands for self-government could be heard regularly.

The British government waffled on the issue until, in 1838, Lord Melbourne turned to the man who had helped pass the Reform Act of 1832, Radical Jack Durham, to fashion a policy that would settle the question. The Durham Report, issued in 1839, proved to be a momentous document, though it was not accepted as official policy until 1846, when Prime Minister Lord John Russell, Durham's brother-in-law, finally put it into practice. The report recommended that the white colonies of settlement be regarded as extensions of British society and of the British state, and as such, could be seen as comprised of people entirely capable of governing themselves. White settlers, as merely displaced Britons, could be counted on to remain loyal to their queen and country and therefore need not be ruled by coercion from the metropole. As responsible members of the British Empire, they should be permitted to form their own governments, the governor-general—formerly appointed by and answerable to the queen's government—now answerable to the elected legislatures of the white colonies. The acceptance of the Durham Report meant that far-reaching self-government—leaving only the power to conduct foreign relations, make constitutions, carry on overseas trade, and dispose of public lands in the hands of the British government—would, over the next twenty years, come to most of the white colonies of settlement.

South Africa proved to be the most difficult of the colonies of settlement to handle, especially upsetting the evangelicals who believed it Britain's moral obligation to ensure the welfare of indigenous peoples. Afrikaner farmers—descendants of seventeenth-century Dutch settlers—had worked the land of South Africa for generations by the time the British won control of the Cape in 1815. A fundamentalist people who took their direction from the tenets of the Old Testament, they had enslaved the local Khoikhoi people, practically exterminated the local San people, and staved off the peoples of the interior—Matabele, Basuto, and Zulu—by force of arms. In 1820, rumors of their harsh treatment of the Khoikhoi galvanized the London Missionary Society, whose representative in South Africa, the Reverend John Philip, took up the anti-Boer cause with vigor. London newspapers soon picked up the story, and the British government felt compelled to act. In 1828, it ordered that black and white men were, "in the most full and ample manner," equal before the law, horrifying Afrikaner opinion. This meant that Africans could possess land, travel freely, and appeal to local magistrates for redress if injured by whites. Worse still, in 1833, as we have seen, parliament outlawed slavery, striking a terrible blow to the Boer way of life.[30] They had had enough and left.

In the late 1830s, some 6,000 Afrikaners headed out on their Great Trek from the eastern Cape inland to the high veld of southern Africa, where they could settle where they wished and act according to their own lights. The Voortrekkers, as they called themselves, journeyed to the Orange River, which formed the boundary of the eastern Cape, settling in 1837 at the foot of the Drakensberg mountains. They then expanded their territory, which they were beginning to think of as a state, into Natal, which the British had decided not to annex to its holdings, despite the fact that a small group of Britons had settled on the coast in a town they named Port Natal (Durban).

The Afrikaner expansion into Natal took place with the consent of the Zulu king, Dingane, who claimed suzerainty over the territory. He permitted the Boers to settle there in return for their promise to kill his enemies, the Basuto. They did so, in a gruesome spectacle of slaughter, upon which Dingane reneged on his bargain and killed a number of Boers. In response, a Boer contingent fell upon the Zulus and killed 3,000 of them. Disturbed by the reports of depredations against the Basuto and the Zulu, the British government ordered the governor of the Cape Colony, Sir George Napier, to annex Port Natal. At the end of November 1838, a contingent of British soldiers landed in the port and took over a fort that had been built for their occupation. They named the fort for Queen Victoria.

The British were concerned to establish peace between the Afrikaners and the Zulus, which they did by imposing harsh terms on Dingane. The settlement required Dingane to remove himself far to the north, giving to the Boers not just the entire territory of Natal but half of Zululand as well. Dominant now in what they called the Republic of Natal, the Afrikaners did not wish to see British control extended into the state. In this they were thwarted, however, when, in 1842, the British claimed suzerainty and ended the Republic of Natal. In response, the Boers embarked on another trek, this time over the Drakensberg mountains and across the Vaal River into Matabeleland. There they set up the Republic of the Transvaal. In 1843, Britain formally annexed Natal to its possessions.

At the time of annexation, the British proclaimed "that there shall not be in the eye of the law any distinction of colour, origin, race, or creed; but that the protection of the law, in letter and in substance, shall be extended impartially to all alike."[31] This declaration, so near and dear to the hearts of evangelicals and humanitarians at home and in South Africa, proved not to be very effective in practice, especially as it pertained to landholding. Ninety-three percent of Natal's population of roughly 300,000 consisted of Africans; Europeans, both British and Afrikaner, comprised about 6 percent of the population; and Indians brought into the colony to provide labor made up the remainder. But a commission appointed by British officials to address the issue of land determined that of the 12.5 million acres contained within the colony, 2 million should be given over to reservations on which Africans were to live. The remaining 10.5 million acres fell into the hands of Europeans as private property or of the government as crown lands. Over 90 percent of the population—Africans—in other words, obtained only 16 percent of the land; the other 84 percent rested in the hands of the 6 percent of the population that was white.

Following the principles of the Durham Report, the Cape Colony obtained responsible government in 1853. Three years later, Natal established its own legislature, in which a majority of the electorate was white. Not surprisingly, voters returned a white membership to the legislature. Just as evangelicals had feared, self-government in the white settlement colony of Natal proved to be a very bad deal for indigenous peoples. As early as 1854, a commission reporting on native policy had described Africans as "savages," "superstitious," "crafty," "indolent," "blood-thirsty and cruel," and "debased and sensual"; it had declared that Africans had no right to the land of Natal and asserted that as "Natal is a white settlement," the 1843 proclamation announcing racial equality in the colony was "utterly inapplicable."[32] Over the next number of years, the rights of Africans were increasingly whittled away as Britons took advantage of the divisions among African chiefs to introduce policies that encroached further on their way of life.

The twenty years of co-rulership by Queen Victoria and Prince Albert between 1842 and 1861 saw important developments in imperial rule and even witnessed some meaningful changes in women's rights. The royals themselves, after a few bumps in the road in the 1850s, had settled into a comfortable marital and familial existence and had won the affections of their people. What the queen would come to regard as an idyllic period, however, came to a sudden end when her husband, only forty-two years of age, died. For Victoria, everything changed.

CHAPTER 4

THE WIDOWED QUEEN, 1861–1872

IN LATE NOVEMBER OF 1861, Prince Albert fell ill with typhoid fever. After nearly three weeks of suffering, he died on December 14. His death sent Victoria into a paroxysm of grief from which she did not recover for a number of years. The first night without her husband proved to be a torture, she having virtually never slept a night without him; her physical discomfort at finding herself alone led Victoria to take her sleeping daughter Beatrice from her nursery and bring her into her own bed. She confided to Vicky that "the night (above all the night) is too sad and weary;" "I long so to cling to and clasp a loving being. Oh! how I admired Papa! How in love I was with him!" "What a dreadful going to bed!" she lamented in her journal. "What a contrast to that tender lover's love! All alone!"[1] She tried to console herself in subsequent weeks by laying Albert's dressing gown over her bed, hugging his night-shirt to her breast, and sleeping with a plaster cast of his hand encased in her own, but to no avail. "My nature is too passionate, my emotions too fervent, and I am a person who has to cling to someone in order to find peace and comfort."[2]

By turns histrionic, selfish, narcissistic, and utterly despairing, the queen felt she could not go on. She found the strength to do so in the conviction that it was what Albert would have wanted.

Her daughter Vicky reinforced this line of thinking by reminding her mother what consequences for the country her absence would entail, playing the "Bertie card" with great effect. The heir to the throne had proved a great disappointment to Victoria and Albert; his scandalous, fun-loving ways shocked and shamed his parents. Vicky used this to cajole her mother. "I can so well understand that you wish to die Mama, to be with him again," she wrote in January 1862, "but who then would carry out his wishes, would work out all he has begun with so much trouble and so much love? You know, beloved Mama, what would most likely be the fate of the nation if God were to remove you now. In twenty years all that causes us such alarm with Bertie may be changed and softened. But heaven forbid beloved Papa's work of 20 years should be in vain. God requires immense sacrifices of you and has imposed such difficult duties on you but He has given you adored Papa for a guide . . . Your children and your people have need of you—you would not have them doubly bereaved when this blow is already as much as they can bear."[3]

Mindful of her duty, Victoria vowed to carry on. Mourning her husband took up a great deal of her time, for few people mourned like the Victorians, and few individuals mourned like the women who gave her name to the period. The Blue Room at Windsor Castle, where Albert had died, was preserved exactly as it had appeared on that fateful day, the queen having ordered that it be photographed so that every detail would conform to the original. His watch, which sat on his writing table along with his pen and blotting book, was wound each day. At Balmoral and Osborne, the other royal residences, Albert's rooms were likewise kept as they had been for the past twenty years. Each evening a servant laid out the prince's clothes and set out clean towels and a jug of water. The queen kept an album in which she collected the condolences she received, copied out poems, and pasted in portions of books that discussed life after death. She brought together all of the prince's speeches in a volume published in 1862 and wrote with the prince's private secretary a biography of Albert's

Queen Victoria and children in mourning, 1862.

early life. Victoria commissioned memorials to her dead husband throughout the United Kingdom and abroad and had built at Windsor a private mausoleum in which he lay in a sarcophagus adorned with a sleeping statue of his likeness. Her matching statue, put away until the time came, would be placed next to Albert's, where they could lie together for eternity. When at Windsor, the queen visited the mausoleum regularly.

In this way, Queen Victoria got through the terrible days. Official work tired and depressed her, but it gave her some degree of purpose. Within a month of Albert's death, she was writing to Lord Russell, the foreign secretary, to chastise him for having dispatched a memorandum to the American ambassador in London without her having first seen and approved it. She also regularly informed her government of her wretchedness and misery, and for the rest of her life she wore only black. She refused to appear in public or to carry out the royal functions her office required of her. Ministers asked too much of her, she complained regularly, unappreciative of what she did do for the country. As late as 1866, four years after her husband's death, she wrote to Lord Russell, now prime minister, about the pain she was being asked to expose herself to by unfeeling persons:

> The Queen must say that she does feel very bitterly the want of feeling of those who ask the Queen to go to open Parliament. That the public should wish to see her she fully understands, and has no wish to prevent—quite the contrary; but why this wish should be of so unreasonable and unfeeling a nature, as to long to witness the spectacle of a poor, broken-hearted widow, nervous and shrinking, dragged in deep mourning, alone in State as a Show, where she used to go supported by her husband, to be gazed at, without delicacy of feeling, is a thing she cannot understand, and she never could wish her bitterest foe to be exposed to![4]

There was more than a little disingenuousness in this particular expression of ill usage, for by this time Victoria had found something of a replacement for Albert. Most unusually, it was her ghillie, John Brown, the Scottish Highlander who had served both the queen and Albert during their stays at Balmoral. Working himself up from the position of stableboy to ghillie, Brown was initially assigned to accompany the prince on his hunting and hiking expeditions. Self-assured, forthright in his speech, strong, and handsome, he treated his employers with the respect due their offices but never lowered himself in their presence. He impressed Albert so much that the prince soon appointed him to attend the queen personally, as we have seen in Chapter 3. To this man, a servant, Victoria gave herself over completely, at least in an emotional sense. Defying the wishes of her family and the conventions and class distinctions of her society, she formed a

Queen Victoria with John Brown at Balmoral,
1863.

relationship with this man closer than any she had ever enjoyed apart from that with her late husband. Although we will probably never know whether their relationship included a sexual component, there can be no doubt that in every other respect it involved an intimacy rivaling that of marriage.

Brown possessed many qualities that endeared him to the queen. Rugged, gruff, and fiercely loyal to her, he exemplified the traits of Scotland as Victoria and many others came to see the country in the nineteenth century—a nation characterized by "energy, courage, worth, inimitable perseverance, determination and self-respect."[5] Scots, and especially Scottish Highlanders, represented to Victorians the very model of primal masculinity;

John Brown, striding purposefully along in his tartan kilt, handling the dogs and horses, and above all, stalking the stag in the rough terrain of the countryside, appeared as the very embodiment of manliness. He devoted himself to the queen, and she felt safe and protected in his company.

In the first year following Albert's death, Victoria became dependent upon her servant whenever she went to Balmoral. He accompanied her on a visit to Germany and, while there, prevented her from being injured in two carriage accidents. This led to the queen insisting that she would go out driving with no one but Brown. Her physicians, eager to get her out into the open air, suggested that she bring him down from Scotland. She agreed immediately, and at the end of 1864—the date, not incidentally, that one of her biographers notes marked a turning point in her relief from endless mourning[6]—she promoted Brown to the position of the Queen's Highland Servant and ensconced him at Osborne and Windsor Castle. In a very short time, he moved from an outside servant responsible for looking after Victoria on her excursions to an inside servant attending her every need and became indispensable to her existence. As she wrote to her daughter Vicky in April 1865, "He comes to my room after breakfast and luncheon to get his orders—and everything is always right; he is so quiet, has such an excellent head and memory, and is besides so devoted, and attached and clever and so wonderfully able to interpret one's wishes. He is a real treasure to me now, and I only wish higher people had his sense and discretion, and that I had as good a maid."[7] Brown ran interference between her and everyone who wished to speak with her, including the queen's children, which infuriated them. Victoria would not consider making a public appearance without him at her side; her intransigence in this regard almost came to a crisis with her ministers when they told her that she should not include Brown in her carriage as she reviewed the troops in 1867. The queen "is much astonished and shocked," she wrote to her equerry, Lord Charles FitzRoy, "at an attempt being made by some people to prevent her faithful servant going with her to the Review in Hyde Park, thereby making the poor, nervous, shaken Queen, who is so accustomed to his watchful care and intelligence, terribly nervous and uncomfortable." She urged FitzRoy "to make it completely understood once and for all that her Upper Highland servant . . . belongs to her outdoor attendants on State as well as private occasions. The Queen will not be dictated to, or made to alter what she has found to answer for her comfort, and looks to her gentlemen and especially her Equerries setting this right for the future, whatever may be done on this single occasion."[8] As it turned out, the death of the Emperor Maximilian of Mexico allowed officials to cancel the review, avoiding what could only have been a difficult showdown between queen and ministers. Disraeli once mentioned that before he could introduce any legislation in parliament he needed to get the approval of "the two J.B.s,"[9] John Brown and John Bull, the term used to refer to the British public. In 1872, Victoria made Brown an Esquire, with a salary of £400 a year, having convinced herself that his family hailed from the Scottish gentry.

Brown provided Victoria with the sense of security and safety she craved, and his devotion and constant attendance upon her made her feel cherished. In fact, she was: Brown tended to all her needs and regularly expressed his complete fidelity to her. Victoria appears to have reciprocated. In 1866, according to a letter the queen wrote to Brown's brother Hugh upon John's death in 1883, the two of them had talked after one of Victoria's young granddaughters had died. "Dear John said to me," she wrote to Hugh, "'I wish to take care of my dear good mistress till I die. You'll never have an honester servant.' I took and held his dear kind hand and I said I hoped he might long be spared to comfort me and he answered, 'But we all *must* die.' Afterwards my beloved John would say: 'You haven't a more devoted servant than Brown'—and oh! *how* I felt that! Afterward so often I told him no one loved him more than I did or had a better friend than me: and he answered 'Nor you—than me. No one loves you more.'" Victoria addressed him as her "darling one" in an 1874 letter, and cards she sent him in the late 1870s read "To my best friend J.B. From his best friend V.R.I." and "A happy New Year to my kind friend from his true and devoted one." Indeed, their interactions resembled those of husband and wife rather than servant and employer. One day, a maid of honor ran into Brown as he carried a picnic basket to the royal carriage. Did he have the queen's tea, she asked? "Wall, no," he corrected her. "Her Majesty don't much like tea. We tak' out biscuits and sperrits." People professed astonishment at the degree of familiarity Brown enjoyed with the queen. A barrister coming across the royal carriage at Balmoral watched as Brown fastened a shawl around Victoria's shoulders. When she jerked her head and scratched herself with the brooch he was using, Brown exclaimed, "Hoots, wumman, can ye no hold yer heid still!" The Lord Chancellor expressed amazement that "anyone could behave so roughly as he does to the Queen." This remark followed in the wake of one of the annual Ghillies Balls, where Victoria appeared in her customary black dress, but this time trimmed with plaid ribbon that she also wore in her hair. She danced merrily with Brown, laughing and happy again. Her family was shocked, but one of the qualities that attracted the queen to Brown was his lack of fear of or subservience to her.[10]

Victoria's reaction to Brown's sudden death in 1883 in many ways recalled her response to Albert's death twenty-two years earlier and her letters about her loss frequently equated it with that of losing her husband. "I am crushed by the violence of this unexpected flow which was such a shock—the reopening of old wounds and the inflictions of a new very deep one," she wrote to Vicky. "There is no rebound left to recover from it and the one who since 1864 had helped to cheer me, to smooth, ease and facilitate everything for my daily comfort and who was my dearest best friend to whom I could speak quite openly is not here to help me out of it! I feel so stunned and bewildered and this anguish that comes over me like a wave every now and then through the day or at night is terrible! He protected me so, was so powerful and strong—that I felt so safe! And now all, all is gone in this world and all seems unhinged again in thousands of ways!—I feel so discouraged that it requires a terrible effort to bear up at all against it."[11] She told her private secretary, Sir Henry Ponsonby, that she has "sustained one of those shocks like in '61 when every link has been shaken and torn and at every turn and every moment the loss of the strong arm . . . is most cruelly missed."[12]

Victoria had memorials to Brown erected at Balmoral and in the mausoleum where Albert lay. Each day following Brown's death she had a flower placed on his pillow in his bedroom at Balmoral, which, like Albert's room at Osborne, she ordered remain exactly as it had been the day he died. For the rest of her life she would not eat her lunch without the two salt cellars he had given her placed upon her table. Upon her own death in 1901, she had placed in her coffin items of great emotional significance to her—Albert's dressing gown, a plaster cast of his hand, a number of family photographs, and a cloak that her daughter Alice had embroidered. Her body was then placed over these items, and her children brought in to pay their final respects. When they left, her personal physician, Sir James Reid, "put in the Queen's left hand the photo of Brown and his hair in a case (according to her private instructions), which I wrapped in tissue paper and covered with Queen Alexandra's flowers."[13]

This had to be done in secret because Victoria's children despised Brown, feared for their mother's reputation, and sought to eliminate any evidence of an untoward relationship between the two. Her family burned entries in her diary immediately following her death, presumably because they contained compromising material. The new king, Edward VII, removed all items pertaining to Brown from the royal residences, including a portrait of Brown holding the queen's mount that she had ordered painted. When it was rediscovered fifty years later, it was clear that someone had driven a cane or an umbrella through it. But evidence of the relationship continued to surface. In 1904, the king had to send Reid north to Scotland to purchase some 300 letters written by the queen about Brown to a physician in the royal household at Balmoral, many of them described by Reid as "most compromising."[14]

Rumors about the queen's peculiar preferment of her Highland servant had been circulating regularly since about 1865, and grew increasingly salacious as time passed. *Punch*, in 1866, satirized the Court Circular in which the mundane day-to-day activities of the royals were chronicled. "Mr. John Brown walked out on the Slopes. He subsequently partook of a haggis. In the evening, Mr. John Brown was pleased to listen to a bagpipe. Mr. John Brown retired early." A Swiss gazette reported in 1867 that the queen, having married her ghillie, had become pregnant with his child. Mrs. Brown, as she was called by an ever-widening circle of people, had then deposited her child with a pastor in the Swiss countryside. Magazine illustrations positioned Brown casually leaning on an empty throne and gazing unperturbedly down upon a roaring British lion. These cartoons, in particular, articulated the anxiety felt by a significant portion of Britons that Victoria had abdicated her duties in the aftermath of Prince Albert's death, and together with the rumors of her liaison with John Brown, helped to spur a short-lived movement to end the monarchy and establish a republic. For nearly five years following Albert's death, Victoria resisted appearing in public, despite strenuous efforts on the part of her household and her ministers to persuade her to do so. She was too fatigued, too nervous and shaken, she protested; she could not tolerate the "noise and excitement" of public appearances, which made her feel "really ill." As the months turned into years, her unwillingness to show herself to her subjects led insiders to question her motives. Her private secretary at the time, Charles Grey, privately referred to her as the "Royal Malingerer"; Lord Clarendon, observing her dancing at Balmoral, reported that she was "roaring well" and capable of doing "everything she likes and nothing she doesn't." Her often violent outbursts annoyed even her physician, William Jenner, who nevertheless supported her efforts to remain secluded by offering medical explanations for her behavior. He understood her distress and connived in her obstinacy and her hypochondria. When confronted by the lord privy seal to be more forthcoming about the true nature of the queen's health, he answered, "But how can I? Isn't it better to say the Queen can't do so and so because of her health—which is to a certain extent true—than to say she won't?"[15]

Victoria did not neglect the business of state. She worked hard each day on the dispatch boxes that arrived twice a day from London and wrote endlessly to her ministers about a variety of domestic and foreign issues. But no amount of work done behind the scenes could mollify a public eager to see their sovereign return to her proper place in the public affairs of the nation. Complaints by members of her household became joined by those from people on the street. In 1864, someone hung a poster on the railings of Buckingham Palace announcing that it was "to be let or sold, in consequence of the late occupant's declining business."[16] It was not long before newspapers picked up the criticisms and members of parliament began to speak of her abdication.

Victoria protested vehemently against a newspaper article criticizing her for remaining secluded and out of the public eye, noting "the indignation and pain with which she read the Article in the *Globe* to-night" and asking the biographer Theodore Martin to try to see that similar articles not appear elsewhere. She was doing everything she could, she insisted, yet "every increased effort is rewarded by such shameless Articles; and the discouragement and pain they cause are very great. This therefore is the return for increased efforts made which cause her painful suffering. Her head is very painful, her nerves are so much shaken and her brain was feeling this evening quite confused and overtaxed! . . . She really is feeling utterly worn out; and does wish some newspaper would point out how much she has done, and how necessary it is to keep her well enough to go on, for else she may be unable to do so."[17]

All this, in conjunction with the rumors of her unsavory affair with her Highland servant, led to new questions about the fitness of a woman to reign as monarch and provided fuel to a republican movement newly fortified by the Paris Commune and the establishment of a republic in France. Some people thought the queen should abdicate in favor of her son; others looked toward an out-and-out end of monarchy. In 1870, Charles Bradlaugh noted that Victoria's failure to perform her public duties had mattered little to national life. "The experience of the last nine years proves that the country can do quite well without a monarch and may therefore save the extra expense of monarchy."[18] This particular angle—the cost of keeping a seemingly do-nothing monarch, her profligate son, the heir to the throne, and a gaggle of royal sons and daughters whose marriages and growing families presented an even greater call on the Exchequer—appealed to many middle-class people. They were joined by a number of working-class activists whose republicanism was more principled than expedient, men and women galvanized by the success of the Paris Commune and hatred for the Prussian tyrants who had conquered France. The fact that Victoria's daughter held the title of Crown Princess of Prussia led the public to assume a pro-Prussian bias on the part of their monarch. For a brief moment in 1870 and 1871, the throne Victoria held seemed to be threatened by a formidable-looking republicanism.

But those who believed in republicanism did not possess the power in parliament that would have been necessary to eliminate monarchy in Britain. And when the Prince of Wales fell ill with typhoid at the end of 1871, the situation changed abruptly. Latent pro-monarchical feeling emerged with a vengeance as the heir to the throne lay prostrate with the disease that had killed his father and the queen held a constant vigil by his bedside. Bertie recovered quickly, owing to an early diagnosis and skilled nursing care, but his brush with danger brought out all the loyalty to the crown that possessed the British public. It became impossible, in this atmosphere, to criticize Victoria, her son, or the monarchy in general, and antiroyal and republican sentiments died away. The queen's image became even more infused with ideas of family, domesticity, and maternity. As the radical John Bright noted about her when colleagues of a republican persuasion criticized her for withdrawing from public life, "a woman—be she the Queen of a great realm, or be she the wife of one of your labouring men—who can keep alive in her heart a great sorrow for the lost object of her life and affection is not at all likely to be wanting in a great and generous sympathy for you."[19] The queen as mother-figure increased her hold on the loyalties of her nation, and, as we shall see in the next chapter, she extended that role to take on the mantle of mother of *all* her peoples, imperial subjects as well as national ones.

Victoria's position as a female head of state created numerous paradoxes within the ideology of separate spheres that dominated Britain's social, economic, and political systems. On the one hand, she was indubitably the monarch, with all the powers inherent therein, and her very presence on the throne provided an example of a woman holding power. The law of coverture did not apply to her, a circumstance that would inspire many women to seek the elimination of the principle for all married women. On the other hand, Victoria appeared to the public to rule not by taking an active role in government (though she did, as her ministers could well testify) but by setting an example for the rest of the country. She espoused passivity for women, a domestic, familial life, not a public life of employment or politics. Moreover, her opinions of women seeking rights were well known. All in all, she did not help to advance the cause of feminism.

As we saw in the previous chapter, feminists associated with Langham Place had made some progress in increasing employment and educational opportunities for women in the 1850s and early 1860s. But the ladies of Langham Place had their sights set on bigger targets: the British universities and medical schools, the latter provoking especial disgust in Victoria. Their activities on behalf of women's higher education ensured that Girton College at Cambridge in 1871, the University of London in 1878, and Newnham College at Oxford in 1879 admitted women to

examination. Anna Jellicoe, an Irish advocate for women's education, helped found Alexandra College in Dublin. The University
of Edinburgh admitted five women to its medical school in 1869,
and, in 1874, the London School of Medicine for Women opened
its doors and matriculated fourteen women. The ladies of Langham
Place also helped to set in motion the campaign for women's
property rights. With the passage of the Married Women's Property Acts of 1870 and 1882, married women secured the right to
retain and own any property or earnings they might bring to their
marriage; husbands no longer enjoyed full and free access to their
wives' assets.

The most radical challenge of the women's movement to patriarchal control consisted of demands for enfranchisement on
the same lines as men. The campaign for the vote was designed to
eliminate the notions of separate spheres and natural differences
between the sexes insisted upon by domestic ideology. The wom-
en's suffrage campaign as an organized movement began in April
1866, when Barbara Bodichon, Jessie Boucherett, Emily Davies,
and Elizabeth Garrett set out on a petition drive to demand votes
for women. By June, they had collected 1,499 signatures. John
Stuart Mill, who had stood for election to parliament from Westminster on a platform that had included the enfranchisement of
women, presented the petition to the House of Commons.

In October 1866, Bodichon read a paper on women's suffrage
before the National Association for the Promotion of Social
Science in Manchester. In the audience that day sat Lydia Becker.
Moved by Bodichon's words, Becker decided to act. In January
1867, she formed the Manchester Women's Suffrage Committee.
Shortly after its formation, suffrage societies in London, Edinburgh,
and Bristol were organized. The four societies existed independently
of one another, but participants soon recognized the need for
a central body to coordinate activities and policy. The London
National Society for Women's suffrage served this purpose. In
Ireland, Isabella Tod established the Irish Women's Suffrage
Society in Belfast in 1872; four years later in 1876, Anna Haslam

founded the Irish Women's Suffrage and Local Government Association in Dublin.

Mill's election to the House of Commons made votes for women a distinct possibility. When, in 1867, Benjamin Disraeli's government introduced a bill to enfranchise a large portion of the working classes, Mill seized upon the opportunity to enfranchise women as well. He introduced an amendment to the bill, proposing to replace the word "man" with "person" and thereby admit women to the franchise on the same basis as men. The motion was defeated handily. Surprisingly, however, another amendment to replace the word "man" with "male" also went down to defeat, leading suffragists to hope that, on the basis of Lord Romilly's act of 1850, the word "man" applied to women as well. Lord Romilly's act had mandated that unless explicitly stated otherwise, the term "man" in parliamentary statutes was to be used generically, including women as well as men under the jurisdiction of the law. After some debate in parliament as to the relevance of Lord Romilly's Act for the Reform Act of 1867, Disraeli ruled that it was a matter for the courts to decide. In the midst of the debate, an MP argued that "if a woman could be brought in under Lord Romilly's Act, so might a cow!!"[20] The courts ruled that Lord Romilly's Act did not apply to the Reform Act of 1867, one of the magistrates indicating that it could also be used to enfranchise a dog or a horse.

Mill's role in the suffrage movement went beyond that of parliamentary champion of the women's cause. His writings, and those of his wife, Harriet Taylor Mill, provided a theoretical foundation for the arguments suffragists advanced throughout their fifty-year campaign. Harriet Taylor Mill's "Enfranchisement of Women," published in the *Westminster Review* in 1851, was widely read and then circulated by the members of the Women's Suffrage Society in 1868. To her, John Stuart Mill attributed most of the ideas he presented in *The Subjection of Women*, published in 1869 but written eight years earlier. The Mills pointed out that the distinctions between the sexes imposed by society were purported to be those delineated by nature, that the private sphere belonged to women, and the public sphere to men, because of biological differences between the two. Separate sphere ideology, encompassing the notion of natural differences between the sexes, justified the exclusion of women from power and reinforced and perpetuated the stereotype of women as "the Sex," making them vulnerable to abuse by men. As Harriet Mill noted, "many persons think they have sufficiently justified the restrictions of women's field of action, when they have said that the pursuits from which women are excluded are *unfeminine*, and that the *proper sphere* of women is not politics or publicity, but private and domestic life." She insisted that cultural constructions of masculinity and femininity bore no relation to the reality of male and female character, stating, "we deny the right of any portion of the species to decide for another portion, or any individual for another individual, what is and what is not their 'proper sphere.' The proper sphere for all human beings is the largest and highest which they are able to attain to."[21]

Harriet Mill did not attempt to deny that male and female natures, as evident in her society, differed markedly. She would not, however, concede that these differences were necessarily natural or inherent to the two sexes. In the case of sexuality, for instance, she noted that "whether nature made a difference in the nature of men and women or not, it seems now that all men, with the exception of a few lofty minds, are sensualists more or less—women on the contrary are quite exempt from this trait, however it may appear otherwise in the cases of some." She thought that the most likely explanation for these differences derived from the socialization of boys and girls, "that the habits of freedom and low indulgence on which boys grow up and the contrary notion of what is called purity in girls may have produced the appearance of different natures in the two sexes." "What is now called the nature of women is an eminently artificial thing," insisted her husband. "What women are is what we have required them to be."[22]

Harriet Mill suggested that separate sphere ideology camouflaged and made palatable a system of unequal power relationships. The designation of "self-will and self-assertion" as "manly
virtues," and those of "abnegation of self, patience, resignation,
and submission to power" as "the duties and graces required
of women," she maintained, meant in reality "that power makes
itself the centre of moral obligation, and that a man likes to have
his own will, but does not like that his domestic companion
should have a will different from his." The so-called influence of
women within the private sphere, stemming from their special
morality and purity, Mill contended, concealed a distinct lack of
power to determine their lives. "What is wanted for women," she
declared, "is equal rights, equal admission to all social privileges;
not a position apart, a sort of sentimental priesthood." Women's
dependence upon men, John Stuart Mill argued, rendered them
vulnerable to them; it produced a situation "which in nine cases
out of ten, makes her either the plaything or the slave of the man
who feeds her." He emphasized the link between power in the
public sphere and that in the private sphere. He believed that
society insisted upon the continued exclusion of women from
public power because men feared the corresponding power that
they would obtain in the private sphere. "I believe that their disabilities elsewhere," he stated, referring to the law of coverture,
"are clung to in order to maintain their subordination in domestic
life." Men's "antipathy to the equal freedom of women," he charged,
concealed the real fear "lest they should insist that marriage
should be on equal conditions."[23]

Following the Mills, advocates of women's suffrage repeatedly articulated their belief that separate sphere ideology masked
fundamental relations of power. In an address to the third annual
meeting of the Edinburgh branch of the National Society for
Women's Suffrage in 1872, Helen Taylor, Harriet Taylor Mill's
daughter, argued that the position of women in society had nothing
to do with what were supposed to be natural differences between the sexes. Physical power had determined male supremacy.

"In the beginning," she asserted, "man and woman were created equals, made in the same divine image. God blessed them unitedly, and gave them conjoint dominion over the world." The superior size and strength of men naturally conferred upon them the role of protector of women. Gradually, she maintained, what had been a matter of expediency developed into a sovereignty that increased with exercise, until more physical power established a supremacy that has existed in greater or lesser degree until now. Under this arbitrary rule woman has been more or less degraded to the position of slave; been treated in many respects as a mere chattel, and she has rarely, if ever, been in a position fully to develop and freely to use the powers which God has gifted her.

Men had determined what women were and were not, what women were and were not to do, Taylor stated; woman was now demanding for herself "the right to perfect liberty in fulfilling her duties to the world in accordance with nature's teachings and her own convictions."[24]

Five years later, in 1877, in a speech delivered to the London National Society for Women's Suffrage, Arabella Shore again drew the connection between so-called scientific justifications and the political arguments against women's suffrage. As women possessed in many cases the requisite criteria for voting, politicians were compelled to come up with other reasons for their exclusion. The "great Nature argument," as Shore termed it, effectively dehumanized women, making them politically ineligible. "We are told of the peculiarities of our nature, our conditions, our duties, and our character; that is, in other words, our physical and mental inferiority, our home sphere," she observed. Challenging the "great Nature argument," she insisted on knowing "what is meant by Nature. Is it ancient usage or established convention, the law or custom of our country, training, social position, the speaker's own particular fancy or prejudice, or what?" She refused to accept the separate sphere argument, the idea that private and public issues had nothing to do with one another. "We cannot separate domestic politics from social conditions of life," she stated. "If then we are told that we have nothing to do with politics, we can but answer that politics have a great deal to do with us." Finally, Shore declared that public powerlessness meant for women powerlessness in the private sphere as well. "With respect to the home as woman's natural sphere," she maintained, "it is by no means her domain, for as wife and mother she has no legal power, hardly any legal rights. . . . So that this distinction seems to result in man's keeping the supremacy in every sphere to himself."[25] The suffrage campaign posed a decided challenge to the ideology of separate spheres and the norms of masculinity and femininity it prescribed. It was not yet, however, a mass movement capable of overturning cherished and deep-seated convictions about gender roles for men and women. These ideas persisted and found reinforcement in the empire, where masculinity had begun to take on harder, more aggressive characteristics in the aftermath of the Indian rebellion.

The images of dishonored white women and swift, violent retribution from manly British imperialists conjured up during the Indian Mutiny in 1857 reverberated fiercely in the minds of Britons eight years later when Jamaican blacks rebelled at Morant Bay in October 1865 in response to high food prices, low wages, racial injustice, and the political indifference of the white-dominated legislature to their grievances. The British governor in Jamaica, Edward Eyre, believed that the rising would spread throughout the island and ordered a severe crackdown on the rebels. His troops killed 439 blacks and people of mixed race, whipped hundreds of men and women, and burned down some 1,000 homes. Eyre ordered the arrest of George Gordon, a Jamaican of mixed race and his political enemy in the House of Assembly, whom he held responsible for the revolt, had him tried, and, on the strength of very flimsy evidence, had him hanged for his offense.

Led by John Stuart Mill, a number of prominent liberal thinkers joined together in the Jamaica Committee to lobby the British government to prosecute Eyre for excessive force and illegal procedures. The government felt pressured enough by public opinion against Eyre to establish a Royal Commission to investigate the uprising and Eyre's response to it. Thomas Carlyle formed a defense committee on behalf of Eyre, which included such literary lights as Charles Dickens and Charles Kingsley. Carlyle argued that rather than be prosecuted for his actions, Eyre deserved the thanks of all of Britain for having saved Jamaica from anarchy and horrors unmentionable. As for his excesses in establishing order, they amounted to little in the scheme of things. "If Eyre had shot the whole Nigger population and flung them into the sea," he opined, no harm would have been done, for Britain "never loved anarchy; nor was wont to spend its sympathy on miserable mad seditions, especially of this inhuman and half-brutish type; but always loved order, and the prompt suppression of sedition." With the memory of the Indian mutiny still fresh, the bulk of British opinion tended to side with Carlyle rather than with Mill.[26]

Indeed, Eyre and some who testified on his behalf explicitly raised the specter of sexual violence against women that had become synonymous with colonial rebellions. His first report back to London after the rebellion told of atrocities committed by black rebels that "could only be paralleled by the atrocities of the Indian mutiny." When news of criticism from the Jamaica Committee reached him, he pointed out to the Colonial Office "that the negro is a creature of impulse and imitation, easily misled, very excitable, and a perfect fiend when under the influence of an excitement which stirs up all the evil passions of a race little removed in many respects from absolute savagery." John Tyndall, a prominent scientist, reminded the government and British public that Eyre, "one of the very finest types of English manhood," had provided safety for 7,000 British men and protected the honor of 7,000 British women from the "murder and lust of black savages." He recalled with approval the "conduct of those British officers in India who shot their wives before blowing themselves to pieces, rather than allow what they loved and honoured to fall into the hands of the Sepoys," and appealed to "the women of England" to make their voices heard in this matter. For while British men might be able to look into the face of death, "there is nothing in the soul of woman to lift her to the level of that which I dare not do more than glance at here," making clear allusion to the atrocity stories of the rape and torture of British women at the hands of Indian men. Eyre's biographer and member of the Defense Committee, Hamilton Hume, made the connection to the purported rape and murder of Englishwomen in India explicit. He told readers of "those fearful and bloody acts which were scarcely paralleled by the massacre at Cawnpore." Eyre himself testified that his "proudest recollection" of his actions at Morant Bay had been that he had saved the ladies, the white women, of Jamaica.[27]

The rising at Morant Bay convinced many colonial officials, virtually all of the white population of Jamaica, and much of the British public that what Carlyle had argued in 1849 was indeed true: blacks could not govern themselves and would have to be ruled by a firm but benevolent British government. Over the protests of some of the mixed-race members, Jamaica's House of Assembly and the Legislative Council abolished themselves and placed the country under the direct rule of the Colonial Office. Jamaica, like India, became a crown colony, governed from London.

The characterization of Irishmen, too, took on harder racial classifications in the 1860s after nationalists in the Irish Republican Brotherhood, also known as the Fenians, began to plan for a rising against Britain to establish independence for Ireland. In January 1867, a number of Fenians arrived in London and set off what was intended as campaign of guerrilla warfare. A plan to raid Chester Castle in early February, where the British stashed supplies of arms and ammunition, was cut short by the arrival of British police, but in September, Fenians succeeded in attacking a prison van in Manchester and rescuing two of their comrades, killing a police sergeant in the process. A plot to kidnap Queen Victoria from Balmoral came to the attention of authorities in October; she dismissed it as "Too foolish!" but it seems to have been seriously intended.[28] In December 1867, Fenians blew out a wall of Clerkenwell prison, where their chief of arms procurement was awaiting trial. This time, twelve Londoners were killed and over thirty others were wounded, many of them quite badly. Prince Alfred, Victoria's third son, was shot and wounded by a Fenian while visiting Australia. These actions, as had been intended, vividly brought the Irish question and the issue of Irish grievances before the English public. But they also struck terror in the hearts of many English citizens and helped to sear the picture of wild-eyed, bloodthirsty, savage Irish rebels on the English imagination.

In these imaginings, Catholic Irish men took on the coloration and qualities of other rebels of the 1850s and 1860s. Like Indians and Africans, they were black. In fact, the facial and bodily features of Irish men, constantly depicted in *Punch*'s cartoons after 1860 in simian, ape-like forms, testified to the fact that the Irish were "the missing link between the gorilla and the Negro." Irish males were not men, not by any standard of definition put forward by the British. Rather, claimed countless English, Scottish, Welsh, and Protestant Irish observers in the new scientific racial language of social Darwinism, they constituted a subhuman species, located on the evolutionary chain somewhere between apes and Africans. By contrast, Britons represented themselves as chivalric defenders of a highly feminine, virtuous Ireland endangered by the Fenian menace. In an 1866 *Punch* cartoon entitled "The Fenian Pest," an innocent, chaste Hibernia seeks protection against the scarcely disguised sexual violence of gorilla-like Fenians from a strong, resolute Britannia who, despite her female figure, exudes manly courage, confidence, and the threat of physical force. A December 1867 cartoon showed an apish Irishman sitting atop a keg of gunpowder ready to blow as a woman with a child at her bare breast and small children milled around it. The Fenian threat did not last long, as its terror campaigns alienated many Irish people, but the imagery used to depict Irish Catholics as inhuman and incapable of self-government would prevail long into the 1880s and beyond, when new movements for land reform and home rule came to the fore.[29]

Catholic-Protestant enmity reared its head in Canada in the 1860s as well, when, under the terms of the Durham Report, the four colonies of Quebec, Ontario, Nova Scotia, and New Brunswick joined together to form the Dominion of Canada in 1867. This new, self-governing possession of the crown expanded dramatically in 1869 when the Hudson's Bay Company, which ruled huge tracts of territory across the Canadian land mass, ceded all of it to the new Canadian government, creating an enormous nation stretching from the Atlantic to the Pacific oceans. The planned transcontinental railroad, everyone agreed enthusiastically, would enable the British to settle the "empty" lands of the west, exploit its resources and civilize its spaces, and keep the expansionist-minded Americans at bay.

Well, almost everybody. In the area to the west of Ontario, north of the American border, lived people called Métis, a semi-nomadic, racially mixed group of men and women who prided themselves on their independence in the wilderness, where they hunted, trapped, fished, and traded along the Red and Assiniboine Rivers in what is modern-day Manitoba. Comprised of decades of Indian, French, Scottish, and Irish intermarriage, most of them espousing a devout Roman Catholicism and speaking a rich patois of French, Cree, Chippewa, and English, the Métis did not consider themselves Canadian, and especially not subjects of the British Empire. They lived in close proximity to the only European settlement west of Ontario, the Red River colony, a frontier outpost settled mostly by Scots. At Fort Garry (modern-day Winnipeg), traders carried out a vibrant commerce; along the Red River for some 20 miles or so, farmers homesteaded and established an Anglo-Saxon community very like they would have found at home in Britain. The two communities clashed with one another on a fairly regular basis, the Anglo-Saxon settlers distrusting the Métis as violent, liquor-fuelled, dangerous Catholic aliens, and the Métis regarding the Anglo-Saxons as agents of an expansionist empire that sought to put an end to their way of life. When they learned in 1869 that the Red River colony was now to be governed by a new authority based in Ottawa, their fears appeared to have come true.

The new Canadian government had decided that westward expansion would take place from the jumping-off point of the Red River settlement, which, it determined, needed to be reinforced by the addition of more Anglo-Saxons sent out from Ontario who would serve as a counterweight to the Métis, the Americans, and the French Canadian Catholic missions. It sent out a party of military surveyors to determine the best possible sites for the new settlers, a step the Métis seized upon to make known their resentment. Fully aware that new settlement would mean an end of the openness of the prairie and the hunting, fishing, and trapping that undergirded the Métis lifestyle, a number of them accosted a surveying party outside of Fort Garry. Their leader, a feisty, buckskin-clad young man named Louis Riel, whose father was half French and half Indian and whose mother was a Frenchwoman, stepped on the surveying chain held by one soldier and announced, "You go no further."[30]

Riel, an ardent Catholic and fiery activist, mustered a militia force to prevent the arrival of the newly appointed lieutenant-governor of the North-West Territories, as the area had come to be called, William MacDougall. MacDougall despised Catholics and half-breeds, as he styled the Métis, and determined that they would come under the rule of the new Canadian government. When he arrived at the boundary of the new province, Riel's people handed him a paper that decreed, "*Le Comité National des Métis de la Rivière Rouge intime à Monsieur McDougall l'ordre de ne pas entrer sur le Territoire du Nord-Ouest sans une permission spéciale de ce Comité*—The National Committee of the Red River Métis notifies Mr. McDougall [sic] of the order that he is not to enter the North-West Territories without special permission

from the Committee."[31] In the meantime, Riel and a hundred followers had ridden to Fort Garry and seized authority, assuring
people there that they were not rebelling against Canadian or
British rule but simply seeking to negotiate the terms by which
the area would be incorporated into the new confederation of
Canada. To that end, Riel called a convention made up of both
English-speaking and French-speaking members; when some of
the Anglo-Saxon settlers protested, he threw seventy of them in
the stockade. The Métis having successfully established their
control over Red River, MacDougall slunk back to Ottawa.

From London, colonial authorities urged restraint upon
Canadian officials. The colonial secretary, Lord Granville, wired
the prime minister of Canada to alert him to the queen's "surprise
and regret that certain misguided persons have bonded together
to oppose by force the entry of the future Lieutenant Government into Her Majesty's settlements on Red River. Her Majesty
does not distrust the loyalty of Her subjects in these settlements,
and can only ascribe to misunderstanding or misrepresentation
their opposition to a change which is plainly for their advantage.
She relies on your Government for using every effort to explain
whatever is misunderstood, to ascertain the wants and to concil-
iate the good will of the Red River Settlers." Despite what the
public might think, Victoria did indeed keep abreast of affairs both
at home and in the empire, so it is likely that she was fully aware
of the budding rebellion in her far-off dominion. All the same, the
rest of the colonial secretary's message delivered in diplomacy-
speak in the queen's name left all kinds of room for reprisals
against the Métis should the Canadian government decide to
bring them. "Meantime, she authorizes you to signify to them the
sorrow and displeasure with which she views their unreasonable
and lawless proceedings."[32]

For the time being the government chose a moderate course;
the governor-general built on the queen's message to cajole the
Métis into submission. If they followed the orders of the government and gave up the province, he declared, they would be

allowed to go free without punishment. In the meantime, in the convention at Fort Garry, a significant portion of both Métis and Anglo-Saxons were being won over by the argument of an emissary from the Hudson's Bay Company that confederation with Canada would respect all of their civil and religious rights, confirm them in their property ownership, and confer upon them the same rights that all British subjects of the dominion, no matter their race or religion, enjoyed. They were invited to send their own representatives to Ottawa in order to "explain the wants and wishes of the Red River people, as well as to discuss and arrange for the representation of the country in Parliament," a prospect that was met with approbation.[33] Just when it seemed that the rebellion had been forestalled, violence broke out when settlers attacked Fort Garry and freed the prisoners Riel had captured when he took over the fort. A local Scotsman and a Métis were killed in the melee; when the would-be liberators tried to return to their farms, they were stopped and thrown into the brig. One of them, Thomas Scott, a Protestant who was known for his hatred of the Métis, was charged with taking up arms against the Red River government, found guilty in an ad hoc trial, and executed by a drunken firing squad. Public opinion in Ottawa was outraged.

Despite heightened feelings against the Métis, the delegation that had made its way to Ottawa to "arrange for the representation of the country in Parliament" received assurances that their rights would be protected. By the Manitoba Act of 1870, a new province by that name would be established, 1.4 million acres of which were to be given over to the Métis in perpetuity. The act recognized the French language, provided separate schools, and guaranteed existing land titles and occupancies. The government confided to the delegates that an imperial army would have to be sent to Fort Garry, but only to placate those who had been so outraged by Scott's murder, as they saw it; Riel would remain in control until a new governor arrived, and his militia could maintain its presence until relieved by the new force. Importantly, the act did not refer to anything like amnesty, though the delegates were told repeatedly that one was forthcoming and that all would be well. The Métis, it appeared, had won the day, preserving their heritage and way of life, and claiming their rightful place in the new confederation of Canada.

But the death of Thomas Scott had not been forgotten, and the presence of a half-caste Catholic rebel at the head of the new province was never going to stand. The amnesty promised initially by the governor-general and reiterated by officials to the Red River delegates never materialized. Nor did the armed force envisioned to be a benevolent constabulary ever consider itself to be formed for that purpose. Instead, under the command of Colonel Garnet Joseph Wolseley, whom we will encounter over and over again in the next two chapters, the army that rode out from Ottawa took as its charge the punishment of a rebel force. Wolseley, an Anglo-Irish Protestant with a profound dislike of Catholics, a veteran, moreover, of campaigns in Burma, the Crimea, India, and China, regarded Riel's rebellion as part of a Catholic conspiracy to block westward expansion of the empire. His mission, as he and his officers and men saw it, was to defeat these subversive Catholic elements and humiliate Riel and his followers. They looked forward to waging war on the rebel Métis.

They were never given the chance. Realizing, finally, just what kind of armed force they were dealing with, Riel and his men abandoned Fort Garry, considerately leaving open the south gate for Wolseley's charging cavalry officers. Disheartened by such a denouement, Wolseley ordered that the Union Jack be raised above the fort and a royal salute be fired from the cannons he had brought along on his misguided adventure, which marked the end of the Métis resistance in Canada. The troops headed back east, and Fort Garry grew into the bustling city of Winnipeg, from which, as expansionists had envisaged, the expansion of Canada westward went on apace.

It was amidst the atmosphere of rebellion in Jamaica, Ireland, and even Canada that the campaign to enfranchise working-class males in the 1860s took place.[34] An economic downturn, widespread unemployment, and high prices provoked fears among elites that workers might resort to rioting just as unrest in the empire seemed to threaten Britain's control, a prophecy that appeared to be borne out by a massive and illegal demonstration of skilled and unskilled working people in Hyde Park in 1866. Debates over granting working men the vote took place within the context of imperial problems and were framed in the language of race and empire as well as gender.

Evangelicals and liberals had long seen working-class men and women as little different from the people of color they ruled over within the empire. Missionaries, in particular, in order to justify their activities at home, frequently described the working classes in much the same and even stronger language they employed to discuss the objects of their efforts abroad. In 1829, for instance, the Newcastle Town Mission reported that the poor and outcast in their area and in other British towns were "more profligate and more perverted than Hindoos." Ten years later, John Campbell observed of the poor and working-class people of Britain that "they. . . present a population as blind, corrupt, and brutish, as could be furnished from any city of the heathen world—they are seared in conscience, almost divested of moral sense, and sunk into all but hopeless degration. They are in all respects 'earthly, sensual, devilish,' without God and without hope in the world."[35]

Opponents of the working-class franchise like Robert Lowe and Earl Russell cast working people in decidedly racial terms. The "ignorance and passion" of the masses, trumpeted one pamphlet, rendered them incapable of weighing national interests carefully, and besides, would give sexually irresponsible Irish men who married early a preponderance of votes over responsible, diligent Scottish men who married late in life after they had established themselves. Lowe asserted that granting the working-class franchise amounted to giving the "Australian savage and Hottentot of the Cape" Colony the same rights as "the educated and refined Englishman." It would lead, warned Sir Thomas Bateson, to "emasculation of the aristocracy." Earl Russell insisted that the nation needed "independent, thoughtful voters" who could take on the problems of "cholera, cattle pest, the Nigger Pest—white murder by blacks—and Fenians," not working-class men who should themselves be governed according to the "natural order" of things. Class, in these debates, was defined in gendered and racial terms.

But, as the *Economist* noted in 1857 in its discussion of Indian governance after the mutiny, British working men were "preparing . . . for a full participation in the privileges of representative assemblies, trial by jury, and all the other palladia of English liberty." After the demise of Chartism in 1848, skilled working men concentrated their efforts on building up an image of themselves as respectable, moderate, home-loving, and above all, independent and manly individuals. They behaved with discipline and restraint in their trade union activity, seeking to persuade employers of the rightness of their demands by adopting employers' visions of the proper patriarchal family in their demands for a sufficient wage to keep their wives and children. They turned the language of domesticity, used against them after 1832 by middle- and upper-class politicians to deny them the vote, to their own ends, embracing visions of the male breadwinner and the woman at home in order to demonstrate their compatibility with bourgeois notions of independence and citizenship. Their lives and values, they insisted, showed that they were no different from middle-class men. Like them, they deserved to vote on the affairs of the nation.

Liberals like Prime Minister William Gladstone and John Bright used the language of domesticity and, significantly, of empire and nation, to make the case for enfranchising working men. Gladstone introduced a reform bill to grant the vote to working men in 1866 with the reminder that they were "the father of families," and "our own flesh and blood." He wished to bring them "within the pale of the constitution," a reference to the area of early English settlement in Ireland that imaginatively marked off the civilized English from the barbaric Irish. Not a race apart, as conservatives would have them, working men were "one of us," as shown by their adherence to domestic and patriarchal practices. Liberals and working-class men compiled a litany of the qualities that made working men just like them. The fact that they saved money, eschewed drink, and "struggled manfully" to support their families demonstrated their virtue, and guaranteed that they would be a force for stability for the state rather than one of disruption and upheaval.

As it turned out, it was the conservative government of Benjamin Disraeli that enfranchised working men in 1867 rather than the liberal government of Gladstone. In a formulation that reflected the shift of notions of British manliness away from the liberal view of reason and education to the more conservative one of body and strength, Disraeli sought to utilize the "muscle and might" of working men to help defend Britain's imperial interests and to deflect the energies of the working classes away from potential conflict with the state toward support of the state's policies overseas. After 1867, it was no longer possible to lump British working-class men, with some exceptions (largely the poor and immigrant population of London's East End), in with colonized subjects as unruly, barbaric, indolent, and insolent people. Disraeli's "leap in the dark" had made working-class men part of the respectable nation; divisions between them and people of color—divisions between those who were capable of citizenship and those who were fit only to be ruled—became more pronounced. As had been the case with the abolition of slavery, racial classifications and distinctions between black and white were drawn with increasing starkness.

| REEMERGENCE, 1873–1887: |
NEW IMPERIALISM AND
NEW CHALLENGES TO
SEPARATE SPHERES

AFTER 1872, QUEEN VICTORIA returned to public life. Although she had made occasional appearances in public starting in 1864, the opportunities for subjects to lay eyes on their monarch had been few and far between. That changed with the rise of Conservative leader Benjamin Disraeli to prime minister, in which office he courted the queen assiduously and positioned her smack in the center of an imperial policy designed to increase Britain's empire and thereby enhance its status vis à vis the other European great powers. His rival for power, the Liberal William Gladstone, often tried to resist the growing demands of both politicians and the people for more and greater imperial adventuring and sometimes succeeded in hewing to a "Little England" line. Other times he could not, and against his own better judgment committed his nation to enterprises that had far-reaching consequences. Together, the two prime ministers engaged their country in a program of new imperialism that monopolized British foreign affairs for the remainder of Victoria's life. New imperialism signaled the culmination of a dramatic shift in Britons' understanding of empire. Where it had once connoted a relationship of white colonies of settlement, of a union between Britons and their free and loyal kin overseas, best exemplified by the colonies of Canada, Australia, and New Zealand, empire now signified possession of and despotic rule over peoples of color.

Gladstone returned to office in 1867, when a coalition of liberals and working men newly enfranchised by the Reform Act of 1867 voted the Conservatives out of power. Disraeli nevertheless remained active, embarking upon a series of ventures to further his imperial ambitions for Britain. In 1872 he delivered a speech at the Crystal Palace in which he asked Britons to decide whether they wanted to live in a "comfortable England"— by which he meant Gladstone's Little England—or in "a great country—an Imperial country," from which they would "command the respect of the world."[1] As he had suspected, the public wished

THE LION'S SHARE.

"GARE À QUI LA TOUCHE!"

Benjamin Disraeli buys Suez Canal shares, 1876.

for the latter, enthusiastically embracing the idea of empire and expressing their approbation for enterprises that would provide a glorious future for their nation.

When he came into power again in 1874, Disraeli immediately put his plans into effect. His first act was to purchase, in secret in 1875, the shares in the Suez Canal that had belonged to the bankrupt ruler of Egypt, the khedive. Egypt itself did not interest the British, but its geographic position offered the possibility of shortening the route to India, about which the British cared a great deal. The canal had been built in 1869 by a French company, but it appears at first to have made little impression on British strategists, who believed that a railroad across the isthmus linking the Mediterranean to the Red Sea and then to the Indian Ocean offered the best shortcut to the subcontinent. The completion of the canal, however, and its success in attracting a great deal of British maritime traffic, altered the situation completely. Egypt became the crucial link to India: whoever controlled Egypt controlled the fate of the subcontinent. The Egyptian ruler served, at least theoretically, as a viceroy to the Ottoman sultan, a ruler constantly threatened by Russian efforts to dominate the Dardanelles. Russia, moreover, posed a threat to the British in India. The prospect of this alien power potentially blocking access to the Suez Canal caused Disraeli great anxiety.

The khedive of Egypt found himself deep in debt and facing bankruptcy in 1875. His only assets, his shares in the Suez Canal Company, came on the market, and Disraeli jumped at the chance to purchase them. He told only the queen and a few of his minister of his intentions. Victoria encouraged him to act, applauding his *"very large ideas*, and *very lofty views* of the position this country should hold."[2] He had to move quickly, before any other company or government could upstage him. Upon learning that the khedive had accepted his offer, the prime minister told Victoria, "It is settled. You have it, Madam."[3] Parliament having recessed, Disraeli turned to the Rothschilds for the funds, secretly borrowing from the banker the £4 million necessary to purchase the shares. The queen thrilled at the news that he had won the day, confiding to her journal, "received a box from Mr. Disraeli, with the very important news that the Government has purchased the ... shares in the Suez Canal. ..., which gives us complete security for India, and altogether places us in a very safe position! An immense thing. It is entirely Mr. Disraeli's doing."[4] He still had to explain to parliament his unorthodox measures in purchasing the shares, essentially, behind its back. He had done so, he informed MPs, because controlling the canal was "necessary to maintain the empire." Some months later, parliament agreed to pay the Rothschilds back.

Though having purchased only a minority interest in the company that owned the Suez Canal, the British public somehow became convinced that it owned the canal itself. Before too many years passed, this impression became more and more a reality, as we shall see later, until finally the French company that owned and managed the canal was doing so under the protection of British authorities and the British military.

In early 1876, flush with his Suez victory and in a vivid display of Britain's new imperial intentions, Disraeli's government introduced the Royal Titles Bill, which would confer upon Queen Victoria the title "Empress of India." The scheme had in fact originated with her, some say because she found herself in the unhappy position of being outranked by many of the continent's rulers, who held the title of emperor. It ran into opposition in parliament, Gladstone being particularly unhappy at the prospect, though Disraeli kept those details from the queen. "After luncheon saw Mr. Disraeli," she noted in her journal, "who talked of the Titles Bill causing trouble and annoyance, he could not tell why." They discussed how the bill might be made more palatable by including titles for two of her sons as the Duke of Canada and the Duke of Australia (this never came to be), a possibility Victoria agreed to, though one that could not have appealed to Canadians or Australians, who were never, in the event, consulted anyway. As it turned out, parliament passed the bill with

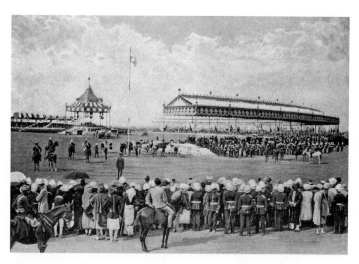

Queen Victoria proclaimed Empress of India in Delhi, 1877.

a large majority, Victoria exulting in it, "as it is," she opined, "so important for India."[5]

As a way of impressing upon her Indian subjects just how important this development was for them, the new Viceroy of India, Lord Lytton, held a grand durbar in Delhi on New Year's Day in 1877 to proclaim Victoria the Empress of India. A massive assembly of 84,000 Indians—including maharajas, maharanis, princes, landowners, and nawabs—gathered to hear Lytton proclaim the queen's new title; to receive, many of them, medals, new coats of arms, and banners from the empress's representative; and to declare their loyalty to their new empress. Victoria sent a telegram to her subjects, asserting, "We trust that the present occasion may tend to unite in bonds of close affection ourselves and our subjects; that from the highest to the humblest, all may feel that under our rule the great principles of liberty, equity, and justice are secured to them; and to promote their happiness, to add to their prosperity, and advance their welfare, are the ever present aims and objects of our Empire."[6] The queen spent the day of the proclamation celebrating at Windsor with a banquet, which she attended wearing the ever-present widow's weeds but bedecked in Indian jewels. From that day forward, she signed all of her formal correspondence "Victoria R & I," *Regina* and *Imperatrix*, Queen and Empress.

Disraeli's new imperialist agenda found scope in South Africa as well, which by the 1870s consisted of two British colonies, the Cape Colony and Natal; and two republics independent of Britain and controlled by Afrikaners, the Orange Free State and the Transvaal, also known as the South African Republic. In 1871, diamonds were discovered in the area around Kimberley, which the generally friendly Orange Free State and the generally antagonistic Transvaal claimed for themselves. The British seized the territory and annexed it, engendering the enmity of all Afrikaners. In 1877, Disraeli, with his eye on the electorate at home and his ear to the rumors of gold abroad in the South African Republic, ordered that the Transvaal be annexed as well. Against the wishes of the majority of Afrikaners, who were, however, sharply divided among themselves, the annexation went forward. Sir Garnet Wolseley, of Red River fame, arrived to take control of the administration, dismissing the president and the Afrikaner legislature and announcing the queen's will that the Transvaal be a part of her dominions in South Africa from this time forward.

Emboldened by the strength of public support for these actions, the governor of the Cape Colony, Sir Bartle Frere, determined to expand British territory again, this time against the Zulus, who lived in the lands north of Natal. Under the leadership of Cetshwayo, who had been crowned king by the representative of the Great White Queen over the seas, the Zulus were a powerful warrior society. Their very presence on the borderland of Natal unsettled many Britons. Frere convinced himself, without the approval of his superiors in London, that they must be pacified if British rule were to prevail. He cooked up an ultimatum demanding that the Zulus disband their armies, reform their system of justice, and permit the presence of a British resident at their capital,

Ulundi. When Cetshwayo failed to reply, Frere ordered an invasion of their lands, sending 16,000 troops north to defeat this mighty enemy in January 1879 under the leadership of the commander-in-chief of the South African army, Lord Chelmsford, a favorite of Queen Victoria's.

Chelmsford figured on a quick and decisive victory. Instead, 24,000 Zulus, armed only with spears, clubs, and knives, divided their forces and drew out two-thirds of the 5,000 British troops that were encamped at Isandhlwana. Some 12,000 Zulus set upon the remaining 1,750 British and allied African soldiers on January 22, swamping them with constant waves of warriors wielding their spears, despite British efforts to shoot them down before they could reach their lines. Thousands of Zulus died by rifle fire, but thousands more surrounded the British troops and cut them down. It proved an unmitigated disaster. Of the 1,750 who had started out that day, only 55 escaped; 858 Britons and 470 native soldiers died. When news of the terrible defeat reached Disraeli in February 1879, he became so depressed that he was forced to take to his bed.

The public reacted in outrage to the news that "spear-wielding savages" had whipped the well-equipped British army. Sentiment against the hapless Lord Chelmsford grew exponentially. In March, the prime minister was able to report to Victoria that he had, "after great difficulty carried the day" against the "whole Cabinet [which] had wanted to yield to the clamours of the Press, & Clubs, for the recall of Ld. Chelmsford." He had done this at her request. By May, however, the outcry against Chelmsford had reached a fever pitch, and Disraeli could not hold out any longer if he wanted to keep his position. He told the queen that he would be replacing Chelmsford with General Sir Garnet Wolseley, to which she replied, "I will not withhold my sanction though I cannot approve it."[7] Rarely did the queen and prime minister disagree about colonial affairs, but the blow to British pride by the victory of the Zulus at Isandhlwana simply could not be redressed in any other way.

Before Wolseley could even reach South Africa, Chelmsford determined to redeem himself. Ignoring ever more urgent telegrams from Wolseley, he marched 5,000 troops onto the Ulundi plain in July with the intention of taking down his nemesis. This time, facing gatling guns and soldiers with repeating rifles, the Zulus could not prevail. At the end of the day, all of them were killed. With a British victory in hand, Wolseley divided up Zululand into thirteen powerless chieftaincies and placed them under British suzerainty.

Victoria decorating officers engaged in the Zulu Wars, 1879.

The threats from the Zulus extinguished, the Afrikaners of the Transvaal revolted against British rule in 1880 and declared an independent republic. The British did not fare well against the Boers, who laid siege to the garrisons and kept the troops captive inside them. A relief force suffered numerous defeats, an especially humiliating one at Majuba Hill where six Afrikaners and 280 Britons were killed or wounded. "Dreadful news reached me when I got up," recorded Victoria in her journal in February 1881. "When I opened the telegram, I hoped it might be the news of a victory. It is too dreadful!" Gladstone, having become prime minister in 1880, chose to settle with the Boers rather than continue to try to fight them. When the queen got wind of this, she protested vociferously to the colonial secretary. "I am sure you will agree with me that even the semblance of any concessions after our recent defeats would have a deplorable effect." She failed to persuade the government to change its position, a circumstance that left her feeling "indignant . . . utterly disgusted and disheartened."[8] Despite her efforts, the British government recognized the independence of the Transvaal Republic.

Facing what they considered a hostile government in the Transvaal, the British moved to shore up their position, annexing, at least on paper, more and more territory—and the African peoples who occupied it—to the west of the South African Republic, till all of the unannexed coastal and inland areas between the Cape of Good Hope and Delagoa Bay were in its hands. This aggression had the effect of pushing other Europeans to follow course, setting of what came to be called the "scramble for Africa."

In the early 1880s, the various European powers carved out large areas of the continent they deemed to be their spheres of influence. Believing that Britain's great prosperity derived from its holding of colonies, politicians and business interests in France, the United States, Italy, Belgium, and Germany resolved to gain their own. Faced with competition for imperial power they had not seen since the end of the eighteenth century, British statesmen and politicians responded in kind, formally annexing

MAP 2. Before the Scramble for Africa

vast territories in Africa—Egypt, Sudan, southern Africa, Uganda, Rhodesia, Kenya, and Nigeria—and placing them under the administrative control of the crown in order to protect British interests there from encroachment on the part of other European countries.

As always, India played a crucial role in Britain's acquisitions of African territory. Ever since Britain obtained shares in the Suez Canal, Egypt had taken on increasing significance in official thinking about empire. The country remained a vassal state of the Ottoman Turks with the khedive serving as the sultan's viceroy. So long as he maintained his power, British authorities were

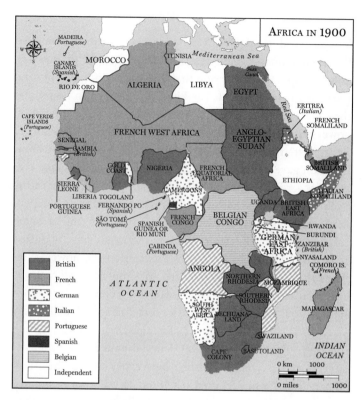

MAP 3. AFTER THE SCRAMBLE FOR AFRICA

content to remain at a distance. But the finances of the Egyptian state proved to be so parlous, and the government so corrupt, that France and Britain felt they had to step in to protect their interests. In response to this foreign intervention, an Egyptian army officer, Arabi Pasha, staged a revolt in 1882 designed to rid his country of outsiders. Prime Minister Gladstone determined that the time had come, regrettably, for a full-on imperial intervention.

He sent an army under General Sir Garnet Wolseley to invade Egypt. Wolseley's forces, one brigade of which was commanded by Victoria's son, Arthur, quickly defeated Arabi at the battle of Tel-el-Kebir, inflicting enormous casualties on the rebel fighters.

The British then marched to Cairo, took it over, and raised the Union Jack above the city. Gladstone and his ministers insisted that their actions did not constitute annexation of the country, only a temporary occupation that would end once stability and order had been imposed. The khedive remained in power and the Ottoman sultan retained the title of head of state, but all power rested with the British army and the actual governing of Egypt rested in the hands of British officials. This anomalous situation gave rise to numerous confusions, not least concerning whether Britain now also had taken responsibility for ruling Sudan, the land to the south of Egypt that had been a dependency for sixty years. British officials in Cairo and at home cared little about the desert country and would have preferred to remain aloof from it. Imperial expansionists, however, insisted that control of Suez required not simply control of Egypt but of Sudan as well. For this was a territory constantly in revolt against Egyptian authority; led by a charismatic Muslim holy man called the Mahdi, (leader), Sudanese rebels meant to end rule by the Egyptians, who, they believed, paid only the slightest lip service to the precepts of Islam. Before they knew it, the British had an armed insurrection on their hands, and they responded by sending an Egyptian force headed by British officers south to defend the rule of the khedive.

This adventure ended in disaster. Some 50,000 Sudanese soldiers met the 10,000-strong Egyptian army at El Obeid and destroyed it. All of the British officers fell to the opposing forces, and only a few hundred Egyptian soldiers survived. The Mahdi gained control of virtually all of Sudan, leaving only a few Egyptian garrisons scattered across the countryside. Gladstone resolved, in the wake of the catastrophe, to abandon further efforts to maintain Sudan for Egypt, a position even his supporters thought unworthy of Britain, and he ordered that the Egyptian garrisons there be evacuated. To oversee the evacuation, he appointed in 1884 a popular and flamboyant—and utterly unreliable—soldier/adventurer, General Charles Gordon.

Victoria strongly opposed Gladstone's policy of evacuation. In February 1884, she wrote to her prime minister to tell him "the Queen . . . feels very strongly about the Soudan and Egypt, and she must say she thinks a blow must be struck, or we shall never be able to convince the Mohammedans that they have not beaten us. These are wild Arabs and they would not stand against regular good troops at all. We must make a demonstration of strength and show determination, and we must not let this fine and fruitful country, with its peaceable inhabitants, be left a prey to murder and rapine and utter confusion. It would be a disgrace to the British name, and the country will not stand it. The Queen trembles for General Gordon's safety. If anything befalls him, the result will be awful."[9] Gladstone held fast to his principles, but there were sufficient countervailing influences that it was possible for Gordon to interpret his mission in virtually any way he wished. With encouragement from a number of imperial expansionists, Gordon disobeyed orders from London and decided that rather than evacuating the fort at Khartoum, to which he had arrived in February, he would stand and fight in order to keep the Nile valley in Egyptian and British hands.

In March, forces of the Mahdi laid siege to Khartoum, cutting the telegraph line to Cairo and leaving Gordon isolated. "Gordon is in danger," warned the queen to the Marquess of Huntington, one of the Liberal leaders in the House of Commons. "You are bound to try and save him. Surely Indian troops might go from Aden: they could bear the climate. You have incurred fearful responsibility."[10] The longer Gladstone's government refused to act to relieve Khartoum, the angrier she became. "The conduct of the Government in the Egyptian business is perfectly miserable," she wrote to Sir Henry Ponsonby, her private secretary in May. "It is universally condemned; and this weakness and vacillation have made us despised everywhere. . . . The Queen feels much aggrieved and annoyed. She was never listened to, or her advice followed, and all she foretold invariably happened and what she urged was done when too late! It is dreadful for her to see how we are going downhill, and to be unable to prevent the humiliation of this country."[11]

But Gordon was playing a dicey, and potentially deadly, game. He would not evacuate the Egyptian forces at Khartoum or even leave the city to save himself. It gradually became apparent to Gladstone's government that the mercurial general was in effect blackmailing the government into retaking Sudan by allowing himself to be held hostage to the Mahdi. The British public, for whom Gordon was a hero, a perfect Christian gentleman who had given so much of himself to the British Empire, would not stand to see him abandoned in the desert by a heartless, cowardly government. Newspapers across Britain and the rest of the Western world, the clergy, the army, and the queen demanded that a British force be sent to save this most selfless of men; the cabinet realized that if the government did not comply, it would be toppled from office. Against all of his principles, Gladstone knew he must act and, in the fall of 1884, requested that parliament grant him £300,000 "to enable operations to be undertaken for the relief of General Gordon, should they become necessary."[12]

General Wolseley assembled troops in Cairo and after months of painstaking preparation, ventured up the Nile. Bertie, the heir to the throne, had hoped to go along, but the queen forbade it. Three days before the expedition force arrived in Khartoum, the Mahdi's soldiers had attacked the city in the middle of the night, killing the inhabitants and then Gordon himself. When the news reached the queen on February 5, 1885, she reacted with fury against her government. "The Government alone is to blame," she vented to her journal, "by refusing to send the expedition till it was too late."[13] In a breathtaking breach of protocol, she sent an uncoded telegram to the prime minister and his cabinet, "expressing how dreadfully shocked I was at the news, all the more so when one felt it might have been prevented." She wrote to Ponsonby that "Mr. Gladstone and the Government have—the Queen feels it dreadfully—Gordon's innocent, noble, heroic blood on their consciences. No one who reflects on how he was sent out, how he was refused, can deny it! It is awful... May they feel it, and may they be made to do so!" [14] She went so far as to privately urge General Wolseley to "resist and strongly oppose all ideas of retreat! . . . she fears some of the Government are very unpatriotic, and do not feel what is a necessity." She knew she overstepped grievously in doing so, asking "Lord Wolseley to destroy this letter as it is so very confidential, though it contains nothing which she has not said to her Ministers and over and over again."[15] Her ministers did not listen and ordered a retreat from Khartoum, a move that outraged Victoria. Upon their return, she reviewed the troops, protesting later to Lord Hartington that "to see her brave soldiers as the Queen did yesterday gashed and mutilated for nothing is dreadful! And to see for the second time our troops recalled and retreating before savages—probably and most probably only to have to send them out again in a little while—is to make us the laughing-stock of the world! For military reasons the strongly expressed opinion of the Generals should be listened to! The Queen writes strongly, but she cannot resign if matters go ill, and her heart bleeds to see such short-sighted humiliating policy pursued, which lowers her country before the whole world."[16]

Victoria despised the policies promulgated by Gladstone's government, a sentiment she extended to the man himself. Her journals and letters are filled with deprecations against him, none more vociferous than those concerning the way he proposed to deal with Ireland.

In Ireland, a depression that began in 1873 devastated a populace still reeling from the famine of mid-century. As prices for agricultural products dropped, so too did peasants' income, until they were no longer able to pay rent for the land they farmed. Their mostly Protestant landlords took harsh steps in response to their loss of income, evicting tenants by the thousands, many of whom then became violent. In 1879, an ex-Fenian by the name of Michael Davitt formed the bitter Catholic peasantry into the Land League, an organization that sought relief for farmers in the short run and the elimination of the landlord class in the long term by nationalizing the land and giving it over to the peasants. In conjunction with a newly formed Irish party under the leadership of the aristocratic Protestant Charles Parnell, whose MPs pledged to obstruct the workings of parliament until that body took up the issue of home rule for Ireland, the Land League forced politicians to pay attention to the needs and desires of the Irish people. The combination of agrarian disturbance and parliamentary obstruction raised the stakes of the Irish question considerably, alarming the queen and politicians on both sides of the aisle.

In 1880, Gladstone introduced a measure to assist some tenants who had been evicted. The House of Commons passed the bill, but the Lords quickly turned it down. In Ireland, a new round of agrarian violence erupted, and Parnell initiated a campaign to ostracize anyone who took over a farm from which a tenant had been evicted. These boycotts—so named after its first target, Captain Boycott—proved successful in reducing the number of tenant evictions by Protestant landlords who could no longer find tenants to work their land. Some of the more liberal members of Gladstone's party hoped to negotiate with the Land League, a prospect designed to send Victoria into spasms of rage. In a letter to Lord Hartington, the Indian secretary, she warned of

the danger, hourly increasing, of allowing a state of affairs like the present in Ireland to go on. The law is openly defied, disobeyed, and such an example may spread to England, if it prove successful in Ireland. It must be put down and nothing but boldness and firmness will succeed. You moderate Ministers must be firm, and insist on means being used to put an end to this dreadful state of affairs. Don't yield to satisfy Messrs. Bright and Chamberlain; let them go: declare you will not be parties to a weak and vacillating policy, which is ruining the country and bringing great discredit on the Government. The Queen does not here speak of what she feels herself, as Sovereign of the country. It is most painful to her,

and she has a right to appeal to her Ministers to uphold her authority and to expect them to do so.[17]

To W.E. Forster, the chief secretary for Ireland, she warned
that "the Queen ... cannot and will not be the Queen of a democratic monarchy; and those who have spoken and agitated, for the
sake of party and to injure their opponents, in a very radical sense
must look for another monarch; and she doubts they will find
one. The Queen has spoken very strongly, but she thinks the present Government are running a very dangerous course."[18]

Gladstone's government reacted to the violence with a coercion bill suspending habeas corpus and permitting police to
arrest and detain Land Leaguers without cause. The Irish party in
parliament resisted the bill with their usual tactics of obstruction,
a practice that led the queen to speak of them as "these dreadful
Irish people." She urged the government to find a way to keep
them "from succeeding in their attempts to delay the passing of
the important measures of Coercion."[19] It did and the bill became
law. Parnell was arrested under its provisions on October 13,
1881, and the Land League was proscribed a week later. Faced
with the choice of letting the Land League agitations cease upon
the arrest of its leaders, Davitt persuaded his colleagues to turn
the activities of the League over to women in order to keep the
cause alive. Fearing "public ridicule," they balked at this "most
dangerous experiment," but finding no alternative, relented. They
asked the Ladies' Land League, led by Parnell's mother Delia,
and his sisters Anna and Fanny, to take over their mass movement.
In London, *The Times* gloated that "when treason is reduced to
fighting behind petticoats and pinafores it is not likely to do much
mischief." But Davitt countered that "no better allies than women
could be found for such a task. They are, in certain emergencies,
more dangerous to despotism than men. They have more courage, through having less scruples, when and where their better
instincts are appealed to by a militant and just cause in a fight
against a mean foe."[20] Members of the Ladies' Land League like

Claire Stritch, Hannah Lynch, Harriet Byrne, Hannah Reynolds, Jenny Power, and Ellen O'Leary, to name just a smattering of the women involved, carried on the League's boycotts and campaigns of resistance against eviction and nonpayment of rent in what came to be called the Land War; they held and addressed mass meetings throughout the country. The queen protested to Gladstone about the "distressing accounts of the disorder and anarchy that seem to prevail," urging him to bring more force to bear if need be. "If there are not sufficient soldiers to perform the duties required of them, let more regiments be sent," she directed him. "If the law is powerless to punish wrong-doers, let increased powers be sought for and at any rate let no effort be spared for putting an end to a state of affairs which is a disgrace to any civilized country."[21] Starting in January 1882, the women of the Land League began to be arrested under laws targeting prostitutes. Unlike their male counterparts, who as political prisoners were isolated from the rest of the prison population and could move about and associate with one another freely, the women, having transgressed the conventions of proper womanhood, were treated as common criminals, indeed, like prostitutes.

The arrests and imprisonment of these women compelled countless others to take their place within the Ladies' League. When in early 1882 the imprisoned male leadership instructed them to drop the no-rent initiative, the women refused, believing it impolitic to change policy mid-course. Agrarian outrages against Protestant landlords increased, a phenomenon credited to the Ladies' Land League. Davitt congratulated the women for producing "more anarchy, more illegality, more outrages, until it began to dawn on some of the official minds that the imprisonment of the male leaders had only rendered confusion worse confounded for Dublin Castle, and made the country more ungovernable under the sway of their lady successors."[22] Their courage, commitment, and conviction put the male leadership to shame, as an editorial in United Irishmen conceded. "We only wish the men had done [their business] as stoutly, as regularly, and as fearlessly," it lamented. "Is it easier to cow a nation of men than a handful of women? Shall it be said that, while the Ladies' Land League met persecution by extending their organisation and doubling their activity and triumphing, the National Land League to which millions of men swore allegiance melted away and vanished the moment . . . policemen shook their batons at it?"[23]

From prison, Charles Parnell condemned the activities of the women, not least those of his sister, Anna. Sharing the panic of government officials over the "revolutionary end and aim" the women appeared to be creating, he began to negotiate with Gladstone for his release. By the terms of the so-called Kilmainham Treaty—after the prison in which he was held—of May 2, 1882, Parnell pledged to bring his influence to bear to stop the agrarian outrages in return for the government's promise to release the Land League prisoners and substantially address the question of rents and land tenure. While presenting the treaty as a victory for the Land League, Parnell had actually given way to the government by disavowing the agitations in the Irish countryside and clandestinely offering to cooperate with Gladstone. Upon his release, he expressed to Davitt his indignation over the behavior of the women and accused them of having harmed the movement. When Davitt replied that their activities—and, by implication, not Parnell's—had brought about the end of the coercion measures and the release of prisoners, he was even more incensed, declaring that if they were not eliminated from the Land League he would retire from public life.

Four days later, on May 6, the lord lieutenant of Ireland, Lord Frederick Cavendish, and his undersecretary, Thomas Burke, were murdered in Phoenix Park in Dublin by Catholic gunmen. Victoria blamed Gladstone, despite the fact that Cavendish was his very own nephew. Writing to Lord Granville the next day, she told him that she "considers this horrible event the direct result of what she has always considered and has stated to Mr. Gladstone . . . as a most fatal and hazardous step."[24] Parnell despaired. The English blamed him, while Parnell attributed the assassination, at least in part, to the Ladies' Land League. He used the incident to publicly declare his disapproval of the association, and within three months brought about its dissolution. Women activists came to understand that if they were to continue to engage in political activities, they would have to do so either as subordinate to men or within their own, separate organizations.

In 1886, following four years of relative calm in parliament over the situation in Ireland, Gladstone brought forward a home rule bill, seeking to give Ireland its own legislature for consideration of most domestic Irish concerns. The queen again inveighed against his policy, "anxious . . . to repeat to Mr. Gladstone . . . that her silence on the momentous Irish measures, which he thinks it his duty to bring forward, does not imply her approval, or acquiescence in them. . . . The Queen writes this with pain, as she always wishes to be able to give her Prime Ministers her full support, but it is impossible for her to do so, when the union of the Empire is in danger of disintegration and serious disturbance."[25] He had little support from his own party either, and the bill failed. His efforts brought about an irreparable split in the Liberal party that enabled the Conservatives to come to power in 1886 and stay there for the next two decades. The Liberal Unionists—so named for their desire to keep Ireland in union with Britain—joined with the Conservatives in the election of 1886 to realize a victory over the Liberal and Irish parties. For the next twenty years, Irish politics effectively disappeared from the national political scene as a sometimes belligerently imperialist Conservative party dominated parliament.

In Ireland, the dream of independence continued to exercise the hearts and minds of thousands and thousands of people. In the absence of any viable political opportunity in Westminster, and in the aftermath of a split in the Irish party caused by Parnell being named as a co-respondent in the divorce trial of his lover, Kitty O'Shea, nationalism took on a more exclusively cultural form in the Gaelic Renaissance of 1880 to 1910. Perhaps not surprisingly, given the prominent—and for many Irish men, the humiliating—part played by women in the Land War, and the continued representation of Catholic Irish men as apes in much of the British press, a great deal of the nationalist work centered on building up an image of masculinity of which Irish men could be proud. In 1884, the Gaelic Athletic Association (GAA)[26] formed to promote and regulate the ancient games of hurling and Gaelic football. Under its auspices, the violent and often riotous melees that took place in these sports were transformed into orderly demonstrations of virtuous Irish manliness. Hurling and Gaelic football became arenas within which to articulate Irishmen's sense of themselves and of their British oppressors.

At a time when large numbers of Welsh, Scots, Australians, New Zealanders, Indians, and South Africans began to embrace the quintessentially English sports of cricket, rugby, and soccer as a way to demonstrate their integral place within the British Empire, the Catholic Irish self-consciously eschewed these games for their own native sports in order to assert their independence of British influences. Moreover, hurling's connections with warfare enabled Irish men to display themselves as modern warriors in defiance of an imperial overlord. A good many members of the Irish Republican Brotherhood (IRB), successor organization to the Fenians, belonged to the GAA, and GAA members carried the heavy wooden clubs called hurleys at the funeral of Charles Parnell in 1891.

Irish manhood as depicted through Gaelic sports countered the various portrayals of the Irish as apelike, drunken, uncivilized barbarians, malnourished and emaciated famine victims, or effeminate and naive children in need of guidance from a paternal England. The muscular, athletic body of the hurler or footballer, the fearlessness required to participate in the often dangerous games—these attributes dramatically set Irish men apart from British men (as well as Irish boys and Irish women), who were shown as feminized or neutered, unmanly. Those Irish Catholic males who had not joined in the regimen of Gaelic games could not claim authenticity as Irish or as men, insisted

GAA founder Michael Cusack in the *Celtic Times*. The "fine, strapping men" of the GAA, Cusack reported, outshone the men of Kilkenny, "pale, emaciated figures, seemingly engaged in criticizing the dress and motions of everybody moving past them . . . Another crowd of persons, who probably call themselves men, was slothfully reclining with their faces toward the sun." The GAA *Annual* spoke of "the instinctive dread of the 'Anglo-Saxon' for manly vigour," while Archbishop Croke, a patron of the GAA, contrasted the "youthful athletes . . . bereft of shoes and coat, and thus prepared to play" of Catholic Ireland to the "degenerate dandies. . . arrayed in light attire. . . and racket in hand" that characterized the elite Anglo-Irish. Cusack described true Irish men as muscular and virile beings before whom an effete "daddy-long-legs" Briton or Anglo-Irishman would have no chance in winning the ladies. In presenting the British oppressors as unmanly, emasculated degenerates and themselves as muscular, virile, and virtuous, Irish men turned on their heads the British representations of the manly imperial power dominating the effeminized colonial subject.[27]

Challenges to conventional ideas about British masculinity appeared from another quarter as well, as feminists turned their attention away from the fledgling suffrage campaign toward other measures designed to alter the status of women. The pioneer suffragists and their supporters had expected an early victory. The defeat of Mill's amendment to the Reform Act of 1867 compelled suffragists to rely on private bills introduced by their parliamentary allies, bills that, lacking government support, had little chance of passing. In each year from 1870 to 1879, suffrage measures were introduced, and in each year they were defeated. Suffragists began to realize just how great the opposition to their cause was, and, after 1870, they tended to give their time and energy to other campaigns to improve women's position in society. The movement to obtain property rights for women, to gain entrance to universities and medical schools, and, most of all, the campaign to repeal the Contagious Diseases Acts commanded women's attention in the decade following 1870. Together, these discrete movements and that for votes for women sought to challenge the ideology of separate spheres that, they asserted, contrary to its promises of protection and security for women, restricted their rights and left them vulnerable to oppression and abuse.[28]

The Contagious Diseases (CD) Acts,[29] an appellation generally given to legislation pertaining to animals, were passed by parliament—in the middle of the night and without discussion—in 1864 and 1866 to regulate prostitution and to reduce the incidence of venereal disease in garrison and port towns of Britain. They gave police the authority to arrest any woman suspected of being a prostitute and compelled the women to submit to an examination by speculum for venereal disease. If found to be infected, the woman was required to stay in a lock hospital (a hospital treating venereal disease) until she was deemed to be disease-free, at which time she would be given a certificate verifying her status. In 1867, medical and civil authorities began an effort to extend the acts to civilian towns and cities as well. The controversy surrounding the proposed extension of the acts brought the acts into public view and set off a mighty campaign to repeal them.

Led by the eminently respectable Josephine Butler, an organization called the Ladies National Association for the Repeal of the Contagious Diseases Acts (LNA) formed in 1870. For the next sixteen years until their repeal in 1886, its members dedicated themselves to ridding the nation of the laws and attitudes that conspired, they claimed, to make women "safe" for male vice and to subject women to the "instrumental rape" of the compulsory examination.

State regulation of prostitution through the CD Acts contained an implicit recognition of the double standard of morality for men and women. With one segment of the female population segregated and ensconced safely within the fortress of home, family, and domesticity, the understanding of male sexuality as an insistent urge that could not long be denied made it necessary for Victorians to target another class of women, the "fallen," as the proper outlet for male sexual drives. The prostitute was perceived to be a depraved individual, lacking all self-respect and decency, and therefore deserving of all the iniquities heaped upon her person by the exigencies of male sexuality, including the compulsory examination by that "instrument of hell," as Butler termed it, the speculum.

The attempts to create two classes of women, the pure and the impure, and in effect to legalize prostitution by means of the CD Acts, in many ways paralleled the conception of separate spheres for men and women. Pure women remained within the private sphere of home and family, where sexual relations between men and women assumed the existence of love, companionship, and above all, procreation, all consistent with the ideology of woman as the angel in the house. The impure woman operated in the public sphere, where she sold sex for material gain. The one realm had no relation to or connection with the other, proponents for the extension of the acts argued. Victorians regarded the prostitute as the seducer of young men, the corrupter of morals, and the carrier and personification of disease, who entered her profession out of vanity, pleasure seeking, and greed. The private woman, whose sexual feelings could be aroused, if at all, only in anticipation of motherhood, would have nothing to fear from the institutionalization of prostitution and would continue to enjoy the respect and chivalry of all good and true men, women were assured.

Butler and the LNA refused to accept the dual concept of womanhood. They objected instead that the prostitute implied social acceptance of an insistent male sexuality. The safety and dignity of respectable women rested upon the existence of "a slave class of women for the supposed benefit of licentious men," as Butler expressed it.[30] They opposed the acts not simply because they singled out one sex for punishment and obloquy, but because they sanctioned the notion of woman as the acceptable object for male usage. The repeal campaign provided feminists with an opportunity to attack ideas about male sexuality, for state-regulated prostitution effectively constructed a particular vision of a natural, uncontrollable male sex drive. By separating motherhood and sexuality, the ideology of separate spheres presented a single view of male sexuality as natural and a double view of female sexuality. Feminists insisted that if there existed one male sexuality, there was also only one female sexuality.

At the heart of the LNA's campaign lay the argument by the leadership that the creation of a slave class of women, while ostensibly protecting the purity and chastity of respectable middle-class women, made every woman a potential victim of male sexual abuse. Feminists refused to accept the men's argument that modest, respectable women had nothing to fear from the acts. They regarded prostitution as the product of male lust, fueled by hatred of and contempt for women. In a society that forced women into a position of economic dependence upon men, only an accident of birth prevented women of the middle classes from resorting to prostitution to support themselves and their children. Their analysis of the causes of prostitution and the purposes it served led them to identify with the prostitute as a victim of patriarchal society. Respectable women were vulnerable to the same forces that were responsible for the existence of prostitution—"the unrestrained passions of men," as the *Shield*, the official newspaper of the LNA, charged in 1872, and the lack of employment opportunities for women. "So long as men are vicious and women have no employment," Butler told the Royal Commission investigating the operation of the CD Acts in 1871, "this evil will go on." Mary Hume-Rothery wrote to the prime minister, William Gladstone, in 1870 that "there is not one of us—no, Gentlemen, there is not one of the mothers, wives, sisters, or daughters whom you cherish with proud affection—who dare safely assert that, had she been born in the same unprotected, unfenced position, in the very jaws of poverty and vice . . . she, too, in the innocent ignorance of her unfledged girlhood, might not have slipped, like them, into that awful gulf from which society at large has long done its best to make escape hopeless." Butler accused the government of conspiring to force large numbers of women into the trade of prostitution by prohibiting them from factories and the professions. She noted that prostitution was "the one trade or profession which our Government appears anxious to throw open freely to women."[31]

In refusing to accept the distinction between pure and impure women, feminists also challenged the notion that respectable ladies need have nothing to do with a subject as distasteful as prostitution. They recognized that the very existence of two classes of women depended in part on the convention that preached ignorance of sexual matters on the part of women. They set out to subvert that convention, insisting that prostitution was an issue of great importance to all women. Butler wrote to an MP that "at the very base of the Acts lies the false and poisonous idea that women (i.e. Ladies) have 'nothing to do with this question,' & ought not to hear of it, much less meddle with it." Such "propriety & modesty" insisted upon by the ideology of the angel in the house, she charged, had been "the cause of outrage and destruction to so many of our poorer fellow women . . . I cannot forget the misery, the injustice & the outrage wh. have fallen upon women, simply because we stood aside when men felt our presence to be painful."

Members of the LNA identified with prostitutes, though usually in a removed and distant fashion. The LNA leadership referred to themselves as "the representatives of the women actually oppressed & insulted by the Acts." Their identification was most often circumscribed by issues of class to a spiritual level or one of sisterhood. "Womanhood is *solidaire*," cried Butler. "So long as they are bound, we cannot be wholly and truly free." "We have cast in our lot with the outcast," she announced, "determined to know no rest until this wrong be avenged, determined to . . . declare in the face of parliaments, and of insolently-proclaimed masculine necessities—'she is my sister, and you shall not use her so;' determined to prove that it is not a law of nature, though these men have declared it and ratified it by act of parliament, that women must be preyed upon by men."[32]

The identification of respectable middle-class ladies with women who were perceived by society to be the lowest, most degraded forms of life, however removed by circumstances of class and experience, was a remarkable phenomenon in the nineteenth century. Sometimes feminists went even further and expressed their identification more immediately and personally. They intimated that what men could do to fallen women they were perfectly capable of doing to respectable women as well, that the demarcation between pure and impure was false. "Sirs," Butler declared flatly, "you *cannot* hold *us* in honour as long as you drag our sisters in the mire. As you are unjust and cruel to them, you will become unjust and cruel to us." The women of Britain, she maintained, "are conscious that in fighting for the injured class they are fighting for themselves, for their own liberties, their own honour."[33]

Prostitution, the LNA leadership asserted, resulted from the dependent position of women. What society defined as women's natural sphere, the home, feminists regarded as a training ground for dependence and subservience, eventually leading to prostitution in the case of those more unfortunate women. "That dependence of women upon men," reported the LNA in 1877, "was taught and maintained by early training in the family, by unequal means of education, by the limited field of industry, whether of brain or hand, yet open to women . . . by every fresh law which assumed or implied the inferior fitness or right of a woman to order her own life; by unequal laws between the sexes as to marriage, property, and other matters; by the acceptance of that unequal moral standard which pardons vice in a man, but almost shuts the door of hope on a woman who has erred; and lastly, by political subjection or extinction of women, which deprives them of any direct means of altering the laws which affect them unjustly."[34]

For these feminists, the double standard, prostitution, and especially the CD Acts encouraged the view that all women were the chattel, slaves, and playthings of men and legitimate outlets for male sexual urges. They made a mockery of the notion of the angel in the house and negated ultimately both the separation of public and private spheres and the demarcation of pure and impure women. Prostitution served as a metaphor for the predicament of women under patriarchal society, carried only to a more extreme degree, they asserted. In the 1880s, after having succeeded in persuading parliament to repeal the Contagious Diseases Acts, many of them turned their attention to marriage, where, they declared, as we will see in the next chapter, many similarities to prostitution flourished, and then to gaining the vote, by means of which they hoped to redress women's lack of power to deal with the grievances they experienced under a regime of separate spheres.

| THE HEIGHT OF VICTORIA'S | REIGN, 1887–1901: GENDER, JUBILEES, AND COLONIAL WARS

STARTING IN THE 1880s, marriage, the central institution of British society, the wellspring of domesticity that underpinned the success of the British monarchy, sustained a wide-ranging assault from a vocal segment of British society. Domestic ideology imbued marriage and motherhood with an element of the divine. The integrity of family life and the guardianship of all the comforts and benefits to be accrued therefrom rested with the wife and mother who presided over them. Marriage and motherhood were the crowning achievements of a woman's life, her "natural destiny" and "best earthly happiness," as one woman put it.[1] Reverence and awe surrounded her position and function. She was worshipped and exalted in literature; poets conferred upon her praise of the highest order. The "angel in the house" enjoyed a degree of respect and adoration second to none.

Victorians viewed marriage as "the equal yoking together of the man and the woman for the performance of high and sacred duties."[2] Marriage was the sphere in which the relations between men and women were said to be inspired by love, purity, and altruism, in marked contrast to the institution of prostitution, where greed, base sensuality, and corruption characterized male and female interaction. The deliberate refusal of a woman to marry constituted a clear sign of her intentions to defy conventional expectations of the female role. But those women who sought marriage and yet "got left on the shelf," as the saying went, realized some improvement in their situation. For most of the nineteenth century, they would have been regarded, and would have regarded themselves, as failures. By the 1890s, with the increase in respectable occupations available to women, judgment would not have been quite so harsh, and perhaps not so readily internalized.

The traditional, patriarchal marriage, characterized by inequality between spouses and the notion of the "natural" subordination of the wife, remained the accepted norm throughout the Victorian and Edwardian eras. Ignorance about sex, unreliable methods of contraception, and the ever-present dangers of childbirth often meant that the intimate aspects of marriage for women could be quite unpleasant. But at least partly as a result of such reforms as the Married Women's Property Acts and the Matrimonial Causes Act of 1857, the spread of contraceptive information among the middle classes after 1876, and the feminist attack on marriage as a trade, matrimony slowly took on a new meaning, one that emphasized companionship and partnership.

Marriage and family life produced untold happiness for vast numbers of people in Britain. But starting in the 1880s, many of the women involved in the various women's rights movements seeking to obtain property rights, education and employment opportunities, the repeal of the Contagious Diseases Acts, to raise the age of consent for girls, and win the vote, embarked upon a campaign to expose the inequalities and iniquities of marriage as constituted by coverture. For them, marriage epitomized and helped to perpetuate the notion of the meek, submissive, powerless woman. It appeared to be "incompatible with freedom and with an independent career," wrote Elizabeth Garrett, one of the pioneer physicians in England, on the eve of her own marriage in 1870.[3]

By the late 1880s, because employment and educational opportunities for women had begun to increase markedly, spinsterhood was no longer regarded as a woman's failure but could be embraced out of choice as a positive, beneficial experience. The *Englishwoman's Review* noted in 1889, "whatever may be said by narrow-minded biologists, who apparently cannot regard a woman except as a female animal, we maintain that facts reveal to us the existence of a certain number of women who, in their estimation, at least, are happier and better as spinsters than wives."[4] The "New Woman" novels about independent, free-thinking, intelligent women that surfaced in the 1890s pointedly attacked marriage in their pages, espousing a decidedly feminist point of view, and even began treating the formerly forbidden topic of sexuality.

Although at no time in the nineteenth century do we find any notion of women's sexuality that is independent of men's, variations in ideas about sexuality did arise. Social purity campaigns, the idea of the passionless woman, and repression dominated the culture until the 1880s or so, by which time the repressive ways of the Victorians probably stimulated new thinking. Starting in the late nineteenth century, in part in consequence of Josephine Butler's campaign to repeal the Contagious Diseases Acts, a whole spate of writings about sex and sexuality appeared. People like Edward Carpenter, Henry Havelock Ellis, and the New Woman authors arose to challenge the advocates of sexual ignorance and innocence, of passionless women, commencing a contest for the hearts and minds of society between social purity and greater liberalization that lasted until the outbreak of World War I in 1914.

By the twentieth century, sex theorists like Ellis had begun to recognize an autonomous female sexuality, though they continued to insist that it was harder to arouse than that of the male. Moreover, it remained dependent upon male initiative. "The female responds to the stimulation of the male at the right moment just as the tree responds to the stimulation of the warmest days in spring," wrote Ellis, maintaining that while the boy spontaneously develops into a man, the girl "must be kissed into a woman."[5]

The notion of passionless women and the interdependence of constructions of male and female sexuality rendered Victorians incapable of conceiving of female sexual activity that did not involve a male partner. Male homosexuality was acknowledged and condemned in the nineteenth century; the passage of the Criminal Law Amendment Act of 1885 made any private or public sexual activity between men against the law. In 1889 and 1890, the Cleveland Street scandal erupted and was quickly suppressed when it was discovered that aristocratic men, among them royal insiders and even one of Victoria's grandsons, Prince Albert Victor, were buying the sexual services of boys. In 1895, the prosecution of Oscar Wilde under the Criminal Law Amendment Act trumpeted the existence of homosexuality among men throughout the nation, raising questions about how one might truly recognize manliness, what role the British public schools played in fashioning masculinity and promoting homosexuality, and introducing a shift in the meaning of the word "effeminate." Whereas up until this time effeminacy had connoted the characteristics of men who spent too much time in the company of women, who were captivated by women and in thrall to their sensualizing effects, now effeminacy referred to men who engaged in sexual activity with other men, to homosexuals.[6] A new awareness of homosexuality among men compelled a more rigid definition of masculinity if "normal" men were to be separated out from so-called deviant ones.

Lesbianism was not only ignored in the nineteenth century, it was actively denied, despite the fact that romantic friendships of great intensity flourished between women. Victorians tolerated and even encouraged these passionate friendships between women, confident that they could only be innocent, pure relationships that were wholly compatible with heterosexual marriage. They did not entertain the possibility that these might contain a sexual component, for the dominant beliefs defined women as without passion.

The heroines of New Woman novelists like Sarah Grand and Mona Caird rejected at least some aspects of the feminine role defined by Victorians and found themselves in situations that demonstrated that marriage was not the haven depicted in conventional popular literature. Sarah Grand, accepting the ideal of monogamous relationships within legal marriage, focused on the institution of marriage in order to expose its hypocrisy. Her characters spoke candidly and without guile about venereal disease, prostitution, and adultery, rejecting the stereotype of feminine delicacy. Grand's Ideala, for example, read Huxley's *Elemental Physiology* in order to learn about how the human body functioned. She wished to strengthen the institution of marriage by shattering the barriers between husbands and wives, not to destroy it. Other novelists treated the theme of female sexuality more radically than did Grand; Mona Caird's Hadria, in *Daughters of Danaus*, for example, displayed an awareness about the role of sexuality in women's lives to a far greater extent than Ideala.

Freedom for women, insisted Caird, was impossible "without the marriage-relation, as at present understood, being called in question." The demand for a modified marriage, whether or not intended by all those women who claimed freedom, was inherent in the feminist message, she claimed. "The spirit of liberty among women is increasing rapidly," she argued, "and as soon as an approach to economic independence gives them the power to refuse, without harsh penalty, the terms which men have hitherto been able to dictate to them, in and out of marriage, we shall have some just right to call ourselves a free people." By the twentieth century, feminist attacks on marriage had become commonplace.[7]

Feminist critics did not object to marriage in the abstract. Most of them believed that a good marriage offered opportunities that could not be found elsewhere. They condemned marriage in its present, corrupt state, arguing that the private sphere, where women's purity and special moral nature supposedly prevailed, had in fact been invaded and conquered by the destructive values and behavior of the public sphere, presided over by men. Society's understandings of male sexuality created tensions within the ideology of separate spheres, rendering it inherently contradictory and hypocritical. In their writings about marriage, feminists borrowed terms and concepts utilized in discussions about the political economy of nineteenth-century Britain. Their critiques incorporated notions of "contract," "production," "labor," and "class," terms most appropriate for the public spheres of men and industrial commerce. Feminists analyzed the terms of the marriage contract, the meaning of the contract for the parties involved, the relative strength of each party in determining it, and the conditions of marriage for women as determined by the contract. The adoption of a commercial idiom to speak about the institution most exalted by Victorians helped to demonstrate that the private sphere of women—the realm where generosity, compassion, kindness, and decency were to prevail—had been tainted by the intrusion of the public, male sphere, symbolized for Britons by greed, competition, exploitation, and lust. By using this idiom, feminists sought to show that the notion of a clear separation between public and private was a sham and to demonstrate instead the public nature of all of domestic life, even the most intimate aspects of the marital bond. Feminists attacked male sexuality and asserted their differences from men in the areas of morals and values in hopes of eliminating the notion of separate spheres and extending the qualities associated with women to society at large.

Marriage, finally, was only a legal form of prostitution, feminists and even avowedly antifeminists argued. "A woman who has sold herself, even for a ring and a new home," advised Lyndall, Olive Schreiner's heroine in *The Story of an African Farm*, "need hold her skirt aside for no creature in the street. They both earn their bread in one way." Eliza Lynn Linton, the antifeminist journalist who railed against "new women," in a series of articles about "the wild women," spoke out against marriage in its present form in 1888, noting that "in the street it goes by an ugly name; but society and the Church call it marriage."[8]

Having only one profession open to her, and limited in the possibility of making the best deal for herself, the respectable woman found herself a seller in a buyer's market, feminists argued. The laws of supply and demand favored the buyer in the determination of the terms of the contract. Although, in affixing his seal to the contract, a man pledged to a woman, "with this ring, I thee wed, with my body, I thee worship, and with all my worldly goods I thee endow," the terms of marriage, critics pointed out, bore inequitably upon the respective parties to it. Under English law, wives became the property of their husbands, ceding to them their rights to own property and to earn money (until the passage of the Married Women's Property Acts of 1870 and 1882); apart from a limited custody over infants, mothers had no rights to their children; husbands could sue their wives for restitution of conjugal rights and have them imprisoned if they refused sexual intercourse; they might rape their wives with impunity under the law; and they were free to indulge in extramarital sex without fear of a divorce action against them. Such a breach on the part of women constituted grounds for invalidating the contract. Feminists argued that this one-sidedness made marriage for women akin to a state of slavery. Within it, Caird noted acidly, "father and mother are to share pleasantly between them the rights and duties of parenthood—the father having the rights, the mother the duties."[9]

Asserting their rights to equality in marriage, feminists demanded for women the possibility of bargaining freely and fairly with men. This necessitated economic independence for women—the ability to support themselves before marriage without loss of status or respectability, making marriage an option rather than an imperative; and the right to retain property and earnings they brought to and accumulated during marriage. Feminists demanded a single standard of divorce, but most sought divorce reform that would raise the level of men's moral standards rather than one that would make divorce easier to obtain. Divorce reform, custody rights to children, and an end to laws that made wife-beating and rape legal—these were fundamental demands for women who would ameliorate the condition of slavery within

marriage. Equal rights in marriage would help raise the institution to a level approaching that touted by Victorian ideologists;
at least it would be a step toward a "thought-out rational system of
sex relationships," rather than "a lineal descendant of barbarian
usages, cruel and absurd," as Caird put it. "Is it conceivable," she
asked, "that when there are, in good sooth, really two to the marriage bargain, one of the parties to it will consent to fetter herself
by bonds which the other repudiates?"[10]

The marriage contract, buttressed by the laws of Britain, gave
husbands complete possession of their wives' bodies. For many,
this issue stood at the center of the feminist movement. "Foremost
of all the wrongs from which women suffer," declared Elizabeth
Wolstenholme Elmy in 1888, "and in itself creative of many of
them, is the inequality and injustice of their position in the marriage relation, and the legal denial to wives of that personal freedom, which is the most sacred right of humanity." Laws that
taught men to regard women as their property, she asserted, permitted and encouraged "outrages upon women, especially upon
wives." Marion Leslie wrote to the *Women's Penny Paper* in 1890
that "so long as in the eyes of the law a woman is the property of
her husband, and can be lawfully chastised by him, men will be
brutal and overbearing to women, despite the most energetically
conducted palliative schemes."[11]

Couched in rather vague terms, the issue that so inflamed the
passions of feminists was marital rape. A husband's right to sexual
intercourse with his wife was absolute, superseding even the right
of a woman to protect herself and/or her unborn children from
disease. In the ruling handed down in *Regina v. Clarence* in 1888,
the judge established the precedent that a husband could not be
found guilty of raping his wife even if she had refused intercourse
because he had venereal disease. Elmy denounced "this infamy
in the name of the wife, the mother, the child, the race, and the
higher humanity to which we aspire." She wrote to her friend
Harriet McIlquham in 1897 that "the making criminal in a husband the communication of foul disease to his wife" and the

overturning of *Regina v. Clarence* were "two of the first things at which we shall have to work when once we win the Suffrage, and they will carry us very far indeed."[12]

While Victorian theorists praised the moral, spiritual qualities of women, feminists emphasized that patriarchal society valued women only for their capacity to satisfy male sexual needs and to reproduce the race. The male design for women, Caird contended, no matter how well camouflaged and sanctified by marriage, remained "that a woman's main duty and privilege was to bear children without limit; that death and suffering were not to be considered for a moment, in the performance of this duty; that for this end she had been created, and for this end . . . she must live and die." Hamilton proclaimed that "women have been trained to be unintelligent breeding-machines until they have become unintelligent breeding-machines." So pervasively had the private sphere of women been taken over by the values of the public sphere of men that the terms "woman" and "breeding machine" had become indistinguishable, she lamented. Constraints on a woman's ability to secure a livelihood outside marriage, a legal system that gave husbands absolute control over their wives' bodies, and an ideology that insisted upon the primacy of the sexual functions of women engendered a situation in which motherhood reflected not "the mighty creative power which more than any other human faculty seems to bring womanhood nearer the Divine," but compulsory, forced labor. Hamilton argued that childbearing was "an involuntary consequence of a compulsory trade." Children "are born of women who are not free," Caird declared, "not free even to refuse to bear them."[13]

The feminist critique of marriage necessarily involved a critique of masculinity. Male sexuality, exemplified in microcosm by the institution of marriage, was, women like Josephine Butler, Elizabeth Wolstenholme Elmy, and Frances Swiney believed, destructive both to women and ultimately to the whole of humanity. "One of the most revolting spectacles still extant in our 'civilization,'" lamented Elmy in 1896, was "that of a husband wearing out (i.e., literally killing) his wife with child-births . . . with sheer licentiousness." Swiney decried the fact that "one fortnight after confinement some men will insist on resuming sexual relations with their wives." Such practices led her to conclude that "men have sought in woman only a body. They have possessed that body. They have made it the refuse heap of sexual pathology."[14]

The experiences of women in marriage, where, in the words of Elmy, they were subject to "the excess of sexual proclivity and indulgence general on the part of man," led feminists to demand the right to control their bodies and their fertility. Yet artificial means of birth control were anathema to feminists, who believed that they would simply allow men easier and more frequent access to their wives by eliminating the fear of pregnancy. When Charles Bradlaugh and Annie Besant were prosecuted in 1877 for disseminating information about contraception, feminists remained conspicuously silent. In fact, they called upon to testify for the defendants, Millicent Fawcett refused and warned that "if we were called as witnesses, we could effectively damage your case." Feminists opposed contraception because they feared it would "give men greater sexual license." Contraceptive knowledge did not become an explicit feminist demand until after the turn of the century, and even then it only rarely found its way into print until after World War I. Feminists certainly favored "voluntary motherhood"—the right to abstain from sexual intercourse. For some, in fact, the right to refuse intercourse stood at the core of their movement. Lady Florence Dixie announced in the *Woman's Herald* in 1891 that the feminist "Plan of Campaign" for women prominently included "rights over their own person and the control of the birth of children." Elmy insisted that "the functions of wifehood and motherhood must remain solely and entirely within the wife's own option." But abstinence from sexual intercourse was possible only if men agreed to it, something feminists doubted the willingness of most husbands to do. Their critique of masculinity instilled in them the conviction that only a massive transformation in the laws, customs, mores, and traditions of Britain could produce a society in which women might exercise the same freedom and liberty accorded to men. That transformation, they insisted, required that women arm themselves with the vote.[15]

The last fifteen years of Victoria's reign saw a new, more self-consciously imperial phase of colonial acquisition that Disraeli had foreseen as England's destiny if it was to retain its status as a preeminent world power. Placed on the defensive by the rise of the new industrial powers, Britons responded with an aggressive display of imperial might designed to counter any notion of economic or military weakness. Poets and writers told of untold wealth and unparalleled adventures to be had in the frontier areas of Asia and Africa; celebrations like that of Victoria's Diamond Jubilee in 1897 made manifest the power and glory of empire. Politicians, military men, and commercial adventurers extolled the virtues of imperial power for national health, seeing in empire and imperial rule the means by which Britain was to preserve its international standing. Men like Joseph Chamberlain, Lord Rosebery, Cecil Rhodes, and Lords Curzon and Milner regarded the empire as key to Britain's very survival, the training ground that would prepare it, Rosebery insisted, "for the keen race of nations."

The keen race of nations could get ugly, involving Britons not in war against their continental rivals but in many unsavory practices visited upon subject peoples. Much of British colonization in the late 1880s took place not under the guise of the government but of chartered companies. Men like George Goldie and Cecil Rhodes received charters from Queen Victoria to form companies that had the authority to raise their own armies, build cities and towns, settle territories claimed by the British in the scramble for Africa, and determine how those areas would be administered. Goldie's Royal Niger Company and Rhodes's South African Company, incorporated in 1886 and 1889, respectively, governed large portions of West Africa and South Africa without costing the British treasury a single shilling. Instead, the commercial activities these companies engaged in—initially financed by shareholders—absorbed the cost of development and rule. As one historian has put it astutely, "it was like farming out an Empire to private industry, or handing over the care of several million souls to a board of company directors."[16] Profit ruled the day, but it sat, not uncomfortably, alongside motives of advancing British civilization in the keen race of nations. Smug expressions of the British civilizing mission masked, at least at home, the profound depredations of colonial rule upon African and Asian peoples.

Rhodes was, perhaps, the most powerful man in all of Africa by the 1890s. Having made his first fortune in the Kimberley diamond mines, he expanded the scope of his business ventures through the South African Company. His dream was to extend British rule throughout the length and breadth of Africa, from the Cape to Cairo, as he and others put it, and they very nearly succeeded in their efforts. Goldie's company secured Nigeria, the Gold Coast, Cambia, and Sierra Leone in West Africa; Rhodes sent company armies and settlers north into modern-day Zimbabwe to establish the colony of Rhodesia; and Somaliland, Uganda, Kenya, and Zanzibar in the central and eastern portions of Africa fell under British rule as well. From the north, an army under General Kitchener advanced from Egypt south into Sudan in 1897 to avenge the death of General Gordon and secure the headwaters of the Nile. Only a small slice of territory in Tanganyika, held by Germany, stood in the way of a continuous British corridor running from Egypt to South Africa. When Victoria asked the visiting Cecil Rhodes one day what he had been up to lately, he responded, "adding two provinces to your Majesty's dominions."[17]

The one other fly in the ointment of the British presence in Africa proved a formidable barrier to the consolidation of power. The Transvaal, home to the world's principal supply of gold, remained intransigent. The Afrikaners' impertinent independence could not stand, apologists for empire muttered; something must

Cartoon of Victoria and Cecil Rhodes.

be done to bring them to heel. But however ready the British public might be to embrace the bloody conquest of African peoples, blatantly aggressing against European whites, officials believed, even if they were Boers, was not something it would countenance. Other methods had to be devised. Taking advantage of the mighty discontent of British settlers in the Transvaal, people called *uitlanders*—aliens—by the Afrikaners, Joseph Chamberlain, the British colonial secretary, had been conniving with the British high commissioner in the Cape Colony to support the oppressed uitlanders should they decide to rise up against Boer rule. Rhodes, premier of the Cape Colony, went even further. He and his intimate companion, Dr. Leander Starr Jameson, determined to help spark an insurrection in the Transvaal by sending Jameson on a raid into the republic to overthrow the government of Paul Kruger and establish a new government under British control.

The Jameson Raid started on December 29, 1895, and it failed spectacularly. The Afrikaners learned of the incursion almost immediately and sent an army to thwart it. British settlers in the republic did not rise up. On January 2, 1896, Jameson and his followers surrendered in humiliation and disgrace. The British government condemned the raid, although it had tacitly endorsed it earlier. The queen's grandson, Kaiser Wilhelm of Germany, telegraphed Kruger his congratulations on having dispatched the British invaders. When she learned of this, Victoria sent her own telegram. "As your Grandmother to whom you have always shown so much affection and of whose example you have always spoken with so much respect," she wrote to Wilhelm, "I feel I cannot refrain from expressing my deep regret at the telegram you sent President Kruger. It is considered very unfriendly towards this country, which I feel sure it is not intended to be, and has, I grieve to say, made a very painful impression here. The action of Dr. Jameson was of course very wrong and totally unwarranted; but considering the very peculiar position in which the Transvaal stands towards Great Britain, I think it would have been far better to have said nothing."[18]

The ignominious motives and behavior of the British colonists did not phase the British public in the least. Quite the contrary. People at home admired Jameson for his reckless daring on behalf of British subjects who, they were convinced, were unjustly ruled by the Afrikaners. Kruger deserved to be overthrown, the feeling went, and the only reason Jameson and his fellows were in trouble was because they had not succeeded in their aims. Jameson, to their minds, represented exactly the kind of individual the keen race of nations required. Britain needed more of them.

Although Britain's population had grown dramatically in the late nineteenth century, it was dwarfed by those of the United States and the continental powers, and its birthrate had slowed considerably. Fears of population decline joined concerns about the quality of the British population, especially in light of a growing awareness of the depth and degree of poverty as rural migrants fled to the cities to escape the agricultural depression and of the high levels of infant mortality that existed throughout the country. For despite the improvement in real wages enjoyed by those who had regular work, poverty levels increased during the 1880s and 1890s, and urbanization made this poverty far more visible than it had been when most people lived on the land. Twenty-eight percent of York's population earned incomes insufficient to maintain a household; London's percentage was even higher. Perhaps one-third of all Britons lived below the poverty line. Moreover, infant mortality rates were on the rise. In England and Wales in the 1880s, 142 of every 1,000 infants born died within their first year of life; that figure increased to 154 during the 1890s until by 1899 it had reached 163.

The existence of so much poverty, disease, and death in the midst of such plenty demanded explanation. Physicians, scientists, politicians, churchmen, writers, and moralists believed that cities depleted the health and vigor of populations, regarding them as "the graves . . . of our race," as the dean of Canterbury put it in 1887. The *Fortnightly Review* warned its readers of the effects of urban life in its description of the "town type." "The child of the townsman is bred too fine, it is too great an exaggeration of himself, excitable and painfully precocious in its childhood, neurotic, dyspeptic, pale and undersized in its adult state, if it ever reaches it."[19] The conditions of city life, they believed, enervated formerly healthy specimens, demoralizing them and causing physical deterioration. The solution lay in gathering up the remaining unoccupied territories of the world and peopling them with Britons. It was through acquisition, possession, and rule of colonies overseas that Britain's health was to be maintained. New imperialism gained momentum from the social Darwinist theories that saw in competition with the other European powers, the United States, and Japan the means by which to create a robust society of virile men and proper, moral women. As Lord Rosebery put it in a letter to *The Times* in 1900, "an empire such as ours requires as its first condition an Imperial Race—a race vigorous and industrious and intrepid. Health of mind and body exalt a nation in the competition of the universe. The survival of the fittest is an absolute truth in the conditions of the modern world."[20]

For others, conflict offered the most effective means of strengthening the citizens of a nation. In the eyes of many who embraced Darwin's notions of the survival of the fittest and applied them to the species of human beings as well, war constituted a positive good, an arena in which men could be hardened and those who were unfit could be selected out and prevented from procreating, and thus passing on inferior or degenerate traits to a subsequent generation. Through war, the effeminate could be weeded out, the manly preserved. "The stimulus of a great patriotic excitement," wrote one apologist for war and empire, "the determination to endure burdens and make sacrifices, the self-abnegation which will face loss, and suffering, and even death, for the commonweal, are bracing tonics to national health, and they counteract the enervating effects of 'too much love of living,' too much ease, and luxury, and material prosperity . . . Strength is not maintained without exercise."[21]

With the new imperialism came a new model of masculinity, one characterized by racial superiority over blacks, action, and physical force, and one which recognized working men as manly as much by virtue of their sinew and muscle as by their temperance, self-reliance, and possession of women in the home. The liberal gentleman of the 1830s and 1840s, all mind—morally and spiritually earnest, rational, and convinced of the inherent equality of all men—would not disappear entirely, but he would increasingly be overshadowed by the new man of body, a figure who would most vividly appear in the guise of the imperial pioneer and hunter. Drawn from the stereotypical images that populated the adventure stories of writers like H. Rider Haggard and G. A. Henty, the quintessential hero countered the image of the narrow-chested, puny, flat-footed tubercular urban male that so haunted the imaginations of politicians, statesmen, military officials, scientists, and physicians. He acted in a natural world free of the contaminations of urban industrial society, according to strict rules about class and gender roles that seemed to be under assault from so many avenues in Britain. Like the white characters in Rider Haggard's *King Solomon's Mine* and *Allan Quatermain*, he was honest, independent, and self-reliant, and among "the most generous and chivalrous of [his] race."[22] A gentleman, he demonstrated the qualities of honor, decency, courage, physical strength, and endurance that had enabled Britain to obtain its empire in the first place. Now, if the nation was to hold on to it in the face of international rivalries and urban deterioration, it would have to build up a race of men from all classes schooled in the lessons of the frontier.

The imperial frontier, and one of its most cherished activities, hunting, provided the best means, short of actual war itself, for developing an imperial race. In hunting, the frontier man learned how to train for war. He tracked, stalked, and observed the habits of his quarry; he possessed skill in marksmanship. A man of action rather than reflection, he relied on his senses and his wits, lived off the land, endured nature's dangers, and ultimately triumphed. Free of women and of the society they inhabited, he displayed a virility that town types could not possibly possess, a manliness upon which the survival of Britain and the empire depended.

At the head of that manly empire, ironically, stood Victoria, queen and empress, "The Mother of the Empire," as the *Daily Mail* styled her.[23] Never before had she enjoyed such popularity. Her Diamond Jubilee in 1897, celebrating sixty years of her reign, turned out to be an extravaganza of imperial display. In that sixty years, the empire had increased in size by a factor of ten, till it comprised a quarter of the globe's land mass and a third of its population.

At mid-century, ordinary Britons thought little of or about colonies; by the end of it, they found themselves the proud masters of millions of people across the earth. British ships docked in every port in the world; British railroads and telegraph wires crisscrossed virtually every continent; British armies preserved

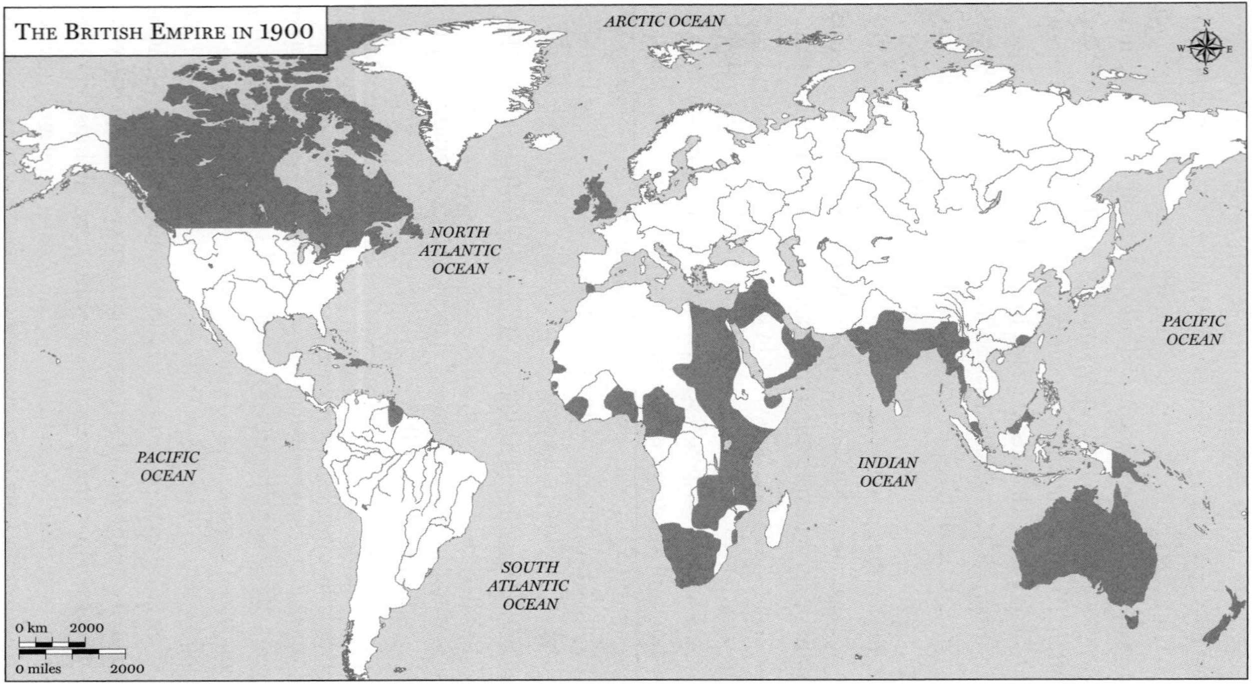

MAP 4. THE BRITISH EMPIRE IN 1900

order in countless cities, towns, and villages; British administrators brought law, justice, and morality to poor, benighted peoples throughout the world. This was Pax Britannica, Britons saw, and over it all presided their beloved queen.

Victoria's appeal lay in her ability to conform to the model of a middle-class wife and mother, an image her advisors and ministers worked hard to project. We have seen her involving herself in the political affairs of her kingdom on a daily basis, but the British people did not know how active she was in the actual running of the country. That was kept from them. Instead, they saw an elderly little woman bowed down with grief, dressed not in the robes of state, which she gave up after Albert's death, but in a black dress and bonnet, surrounded by her children and grandchildren, the quintessential loving wife and mother, the model of domesticity and separate spheres.

The fears of deterioration that informed the writings of imperialists and social Darwinists were confirmed and exacerbated in the very last years of the nineteenth century when Britain provoked a war against the small but determined group of Dutch Afrikaner farmers—called Boers in the parlance of the time--in the Transvaal in South Africa in 1899 in order to secure its hold on the gold mines of the Rand. Confident of their success and determined to teach the Boers a lesson about the power and glory of the British Empire, politicians and the public were stunned when their armies suffered a series of humiliating and embarrassing defeats in the first months of the war. By late 1900, those losses had been reversed, but the defeat of the 45,000 Afrikaner guerrilla soldiers required an additional eighteen months and 450,000 British soldiers.

Britons believed war with the Boers to be inevitable. As Winston Churchill had put it, "sooner or later, in a righteous cause or a picked quarrel . . . for the sake of our Empire, for the sake of our honour, for the sake of the race, we must fight the Boers."[24] It was really for the sake of the gold mines in the Transvaal Republic, but no matter. The presence of so many Britons in the

Boer Republic, where they constituted a majority of the population, paid 80 percent of the taxes, and yet had no rights of citizenship, provided the righteous cause. As Victoria wrote to the young queen of the Netherlands, "I cannot abandon my own subjects who have appealed to me for protection."[25] The picked quarrel, ironically, came from the Boers themselves, who after the Jameson Raid saw the writing on the wall and felt they had to move quickly if they were to have any chance of preventing a British takeover of their country. On October 11, 1899, they launched what they regarded as a preventive invasion of the Natal province and the Cape Colony. Before a week passed, three divisions of British troops had embarked on their voyage to destroy the Boers and gain fame and glory for themselves and for their queen. She had inspected the Gordon Highlanders before they left and described in her journal the "very touching" occasion. "I felt quite a lump in my throat as we drove away, and I thought of how these remarkably fine men might not all return."[26]

An understatement if there ever was one. For all the talk of the need to prepare for the keen race of nations, British planners had done little to modernize their army. In its attitudes and tactics, it harkened back to the days of Wellington. It might possess modern arms—machine guns and repeater rifles—but it employed them in decidedly ancient ways. Soldiers went into battle led by pipers and drummers, and only recently had they shed their redcoats for a drabber olive uniform. They formed up in battle squares and advanced in close order. Moreover, they had not fought Europeans since the Crimean War in the 1850s, except for meeting the Boers in the debacle at Majuba Hill in 1881, when they had been utterly humiliated.

The Boers, in many ways, looked precisely like those imperial pioneers and hunters extolled in British adventure stories. They constituted not an army per se as much as an irregular commando force made up of virtually all Afrikaner men, showing up when they felt it necessary—and departing when they had more pressing issues elsewhere—on the backs of their own horses in homespun clothing that barely resembled anything like a uniform. Their discipline was lax and they elected their own officers. But in addition to the modern weapons they brought to the battlefield, they possessed extraordinary skills of horsemanship and knew the terrain like the backs of their hands. Consummate hunters, they responded to the needs of the moment, flexible in their tactics and responsive to whatever the situation they faced might demand. They knew what they were doing in defense of their land and their way of life.

Despite being heavily outnumbered, the Boers inflicted a series of losses on the British forces. After the first of such defeats, at Glencoe, the queen told the secretary for war, Lord Lansdowne, that "my heart bleeds for these dreadful losses." By December, she was recording in her journal that Lansdowne was "depressed," and General Wolseley "much annoyed with the Generals, who he considers have not done what they were advised to do, but have attacked difficult and inaccessible positions, instead of trying to outflank the enemy."[27] During a particularly bad spell in December 1899, which came to be called Black Week, A. J. Balfour, first lord of the treasury, paid a visit to Victoria to apprise her of the dire situation. "Please understand," she instructed him, "that there is no depression in *this* house; we are not interested in the possibilities of defeat; they do not exist."[28] But she was deeply afflicted by the losses of her soldiers, writing to their widows and mothers and keeping an album in which she pasted pictures of every officer killed in the war, one of which was that of her own grandson, Prince Christian Victor, who died of tropical fever. She knit woolen caps and comforters and had sent to every British soldier and officer at Christmastime a box of chocolates with her image on the cover.

The British performance in the first months of the war proved so inept that calls for an inquiry soon arose. Victoria cautioned against it, telling her prime minister, Lord Salisbury, that it must wait until the war ended. "It would only be repeated back to the Boers and to foreign countries," she noted, "and would do us a great deal of harm." She urged instead that more troops be sent as quickly as possible and advised that any bureaucratic barriers to rapid mobilization be dispensed with immediately as "useless difficulties." "The loss of so many valuable lives for nothing is terrible," she insisted, and she was "determined to press any available measure to put us in a safe position, and to put an end to these terrible failures."[29]

The terrible failures started to turn around in February 1900 with the relief of two towns, Kimberley and Ladysmith. The queen fired off telegrams of congratulations to her generals. In the scheme of things, these victories should have been accepted as a matter of course, but so bad had the situation been just a

Women and children transported to camps during South African War, 1901.

month earlier that the British public erupted in wild celebration. Victoria traveled by carriage through London, cheered on by thousands of her subjects waving Union Jacks and singing "God Save the Queen." "It was like a triumphal progress," she reported of the huge crowds that surpassed even those of her Diamond Jubilee.[30] The disproportionate response to the victory demonstrates just how bad things had gotten.

The war continued, the fighting bitter and ugly and seemingly endless. Britain carried out a scorched earth policy, firing farmhouses and fields. Both sides executed prisoners in the field, ignoring international rules governing warfare. The British threw women and children into concentration camps, the first the world had seen, whose terrible conditions left their inmates diseased and malnourished. Twenty-two thousand Britons died, two-thirds of them from disease. Twenty-four thousand Afrikaners died, 20,000 of them women and children who had suffered in the camps. The remaining Afrikaners found themselves destitute and nearly starved when the fighting stopped in May 1902.

Funeral of Queen Victoria, 1901.

Queen Victoria did not see its end. She died on January 22, 1901. A week earlier, she had seen her last nonfamily visitor, Field Marshall Lord Roberts, with whom she spoke about the progress of the war. She believed that its stresses had created the ill health in which she now found herself. On January 19, she was glad to hear that "there is much better news from South Africa today."[31] Upon her death, as she had long insisted as commander in chief of the nation's armed forces, she was given a military funeral. The war dragged on for another sixteen months after she was gone, its grubby victory leaving Britons with a very bad taste in their mouths.

The Peace of Vereeniging concluding the conflict was a generous one, designed to reconcile the Boers to membership in a union of the four colonies of South Africa. The treaty compensated the Transvaal for the devastation it had suffered, guaranteed full equality within the union, and recognized the Afrikaner language. The British hoped that their magnanimity would enable them to establish a secure Union of South Africa dominated by British citizens who could control the gold fields and provide some degree of protection of Africans from Afrikaners. The Boers saw the arrangement differently, seeing in a self-governing Union of South Africa the possibility of their gaining the upper hand over all the constituent parts, thus asserting their own control of the wealth and the African peoples of the land. They were right, as it turned out.

CHAPTER 7

|THE LEGACY OF THE LATE QUEEN|

THE PERIOD WE CALL VICTORIAN and many of the values associated with it came to an end with the death of the queen. In reality, those values had been under attack for some time before she died, but her passing marked a definitive moment in the lives of contemporaries. The great queen was dead. It seemed impossible, for she had always been there. What would national life be like without her?

The new king, Edward VII, symbolized for many the changes that lay ahead. Where Victoria—the mother of the nation—had been sober, serious-minded, and censorious at times, he seemed to be the fun uncle who came to visit, instigated his nieces and nephews in raucous play, and then left when the cleaning up had to be done. The appearance of economic prosperity (which would prove to be based on unstable foundations) and a new cultural vibrancy we associate with modernism only made the contrast of the Edwardian to the Victorian era all the more stark.

The queen's death and the Boer War marked a turning point in Britain's relationship with empire. The braggadocio and high emotion that had characterized the last quarter of the nineteenth century cooled considerably under the impact of the realization that a bunch of farmers whose numbers came to about half the population of Birmingham had reduced Britain to a third-rate power, as A. J. Balfour, the new prime minister, put it publicly.[1]

The British did not lose their taste for empire, and indeed, would expand it considerably following World War I, but the jingoism and expressions of glory did not survive the catastrophe of the Boer War.

In the process of recruiting soldiers for the war, British officials discovered that fully one-third of those who sought to enlist did not meet military standards of physical health.[2] They were too short, suffered from heart trouble or rheumatism, had weak lungs or flat feet or bad teeth. The small-chested "New Town Type" could not stand up to the rigors of physical training and war, and even many of those who passed through the initial screening had to leave the army later when their health failed. Major General Frederick Maurice reckoned in 1903 that when both the first rejections and the subsequent dropouts were counted, only two of every five volunteers had proved to be competent soldiers. These figures promised disaster, he warned, for "no nation was ever yet for any long time great and free when the army it put into the field no longer represented its own virility and manhood."[3] When compared to the Germans—indeed even to the Boers and the Japanese—the British race of men paled. Near panic about race degeneration, physical degeneration, and deterioration ensued.

Major General Maurice and other military and civilian officials assigned responsibility for the deficiencies they found in the rejected recruits for the Boer War to mothers of the working classes. "Whatever the primary cause," Maurice declared, "the young man of 16 or 18 years of age is what he is because of the training through which he has passed during his infancy and childhood . . . Therefore it is to the condition, mental, moral, and physical, of the women and children that we must look if we have regard to the future of our land." The Inter-Departmental Committee on Physical Deterioration, reporting in 1904, and a number of other parliamentary committees stressed the ignorance and fecklessness of mothers as a factor in the physical decline of the population, blaming mothers for making their children sick.

Maurice suggested that Britons might learn from the Germans how to raise "a virile race, either of soldiers or of citizens." The one essential ingredient, he observed, was that "the attention of the mothers of a land should be mainly devoted to the three K's— Kinder, Kuche, Kirche [Children, Kitchen, Church]." Others looked to practices in Japan, which was "in no danger of race-suicide." They proposed a series of reforms that would compel mothers to learn "mothercraft" in order to improve the health and welfare of their children, and thus the health and welfare of the state.[4]

A spate of child welfare provisions followed. In 1906, an education act providing for meals for poor London schoolchildren was enacted; another in 1907 required children to undergo medical inspection. The 1907 Notification of Births Act mandated that fathers or those attending deliveries register all live births with the local authorities within thirty-six hours; midwives required training. The 1908 Children Act set up a separate system of justice for youths, made it illegal for children under fourteen to enter pubs, criminalized the "overlaying" (suffocation) of children if the adult was drunk at the time he or she went to bed, and provided punishments if a child died for lack of fireguards in the home. In keeping with the often punitive tone and substance of the infant welfare movement, much of it directed at women, the Children Act identified and penalized for the first time the neglect of children by their parents.

Contrary to liberal convictions that the individual should operate free of interference from or compulsion by the state, the infant welfare movement of the early twentieth century imposed on individuals—and in this case, particular individuals, mothers— to address and resolve national problems of public health, domestic politics, and imperial and international conflict. The raising of children now became a national obligation on the part of women,[5] rather than a moral or social duty, and if they did not perform this function adequately, the state would step in to insist that they do it better. Wholly ignoring the environmental factors working-class families faced—poverty, overcrowding, unsanitary streets, water and sewage systems, pollution, epidemic and chronic disease—the state conferred upon women who had no control over them the responsibility, but not the resources, to improve the stock of the nation. And, operating according to a largely negative set of images of working-class women, state officials and voluntary agencies like the Charity Organization Society turned to laws that coerced mothers into providing a certain kind and level of care, rather than legislation designed to help them by providing the necessary means. As working-class women saw it, reformers were requiring them to reallocate scarce resources from one part of the family to another. This situation demanded, given the tradition of husbands keeping a part of their pay packet for themselves to buy tobacco and drink and giving the remainder to their wives to manage as best they could, that women themselves go without food, clothing, rest, and good health so that the new state requirements for their children could be met. And if they were not, working-class mothers faced countless humiliations from officious, intrusive, arrogant, and impolite middle-class district visitors; fines; jail sentences; and even loss of their children. As Anna Martin, a social worker and feminist, observed of the working-class mother at the time, the child welfare movement expected that she become "the unpaid nursemaid of the State."[6]

Concerns about the deterioration of the race and its impact on Britain's power and place in the world were heightened by Japan's victory over Russia in 1905 in the Russo-Japanese War. A non-white people had handily defeated a great European power. In conjunction with pressure from a restive electorate made up of many working-class voters, these concerns about the fitness of the British people finally compelled the Liberal government, which had come back into power in 1905, to abdicate long-held positions about the need of the state to stay aloof from the workings of the economy and of society and to introduce measures that taxed the wealthy in order to provide basic (and usually inadequate) subsistence to (some of) the unemployed, the elderly, and the sick. In 1908, the chancellor of the exchequer, Herbert Henry Asquith, included a plan to provide old-age pensions in the budget. The sums prescribed were small and limited to those who had earned a certain level of income before they turned seventy, but some 1 million elderly immediately benefited from them, and their provision marked an unprecedented departure from classical liberal principles. Classical liberals believed that government's proper function consisted solely in providing opportunities for the exercise of freedom and liberty; in what historians have regarded as one of the first steps on the road to creating the welfare state of the twentieth century, the government recognized that one of its major obligations was to provide some measure of material security to at least some of its citizens. In 1909, when the Welshman David Lloyd George, now chancellor of the exchequer under the prime ministership of Asquith, presented his "People's Budget" before parliament, he extended this obligation to the unemployed and the sick. He proposed to pay for these pensions and other social services designed to reduce poverty by levying a new supertax on the wealthy; the budget also raised death duties on the inheritance of large estates to 25 percent of their worth, placed a tax on gasoline and automobiles, and worst of all, from the perspective of elites, imposed capital gains taxes on land and minerals when they changed hands. In short, the People's Budget sought to redistribute a modest portion of the wealth of the country from the very rich to the poor.

Resistance from the Conservative party proved to be so great that the Liberal government felt compelled to cripple the power of the Lords, where Conservatives held a majority, to scuttle legislation. By the Parliament Act of 1911—which only passed the House of Lords after the king threatened to create hundreds of new Liberal peers, thus diluting both the Conservative majority and the prestige of nobility—Britain's ancient constitution was significantly altered. From here on, the House of Lords could only delay, rather than veto, legislation. If passed by the Commons in three successive years, the measures would become law. The

Parliament Act ensured that legislation granting home rule to Ireland would be just a matter of time. Dependent upon Irish as well as Labor votes for its majority, the Liberal party had had to promise that it would introduce a measure for home rule the very next year. Its passage was delayed by the Lords for three years, and when it was due to come into force in 1914, it was delayed by the outbreak of World War I.

The suffrage campaign, which had become muted and diffuse after 1870, picked up a terrific head of steam in 1905, when a new phase of militancy galvanized adherents and the campaign became a mass movement. Suffrage societies, both militant and constitutional, grew in size and in number; huge public demonstrations took place; women under the banner of the Women's Social and Political Union marched on parliament and heckled MPs. In 1909, WSPU members took up stones, throwing them through government windows. When arrested, they embarked on hunger strikes in prison and were subjected to forced feeding. Their lawbreaking took on even greater scope when some of them turned to arson. On the constitutional front, little was done. Asquith's government promised to bring forward a bill that could be amended to include women's suffrage bill, but it never did. Militancy intensified as a result, and it is impossible to know just how far it might have gone had World War I not broken out in 1914, at which time, suffragists of all stripes left off their campaigning for votes for women and turned to support the war effort.

For all intents and purposes, suffrage was dead for the duration of the war. In 1917, however, the government became concerned about the need to call a new election, and on the basis of the old franchise the men of the armed forces and those serving in wartime industries would no longer be eligible to vote. Various suggestions for the amelioration of this injustice were advanced, but Parliament finally agreed on the need for a new franchise. At this point, the constitutional suffragists demanded that women also be included. The timing worked beautifully. Steadfast opponents of women's suffrage could not ignore the contributions made by

British women to the war effort and were inclined to reward them for their service. After months of negotiations, an agreement was reached.

The 1918 Representation of the People Act gave men the vote on the basis of residence of premises, a grant of universal manhood suffrage. It restricted the vote to those women who were householders or the wives of householders, and who had reached the age of thirty. The age requirement served to ensure that women would not enjoy a majority. The acceptance of it constituted an abandonment of the long-held principle of sex equality fought for by so many women—votes for women on the same lines as it was or should be granted to men. Apologists explained that they did not want to risk losing a partial victory by holding out for more. Parliament finally granted votes for women on the same terms as men in 1928.

PRIMARY SOURCE EXCERPTS
AND STUDY QUESTIONS

THIS BOOK HAS FOCUSED ON two themes: (1) the contradictions between a domestic ideology that denied women the rights of citizenship and the fact of a woman ruling as sovereign over the United Kingdom and its empire; and (2) the role played by Queen Victoria in the gaining and administering of that empire. The primary documents that follow pick up on these two ideas; keep them in mind as you read the sources and answer the questions that follow.

I.

The first document is drawn from an open letter written by Caroline Norton to Queen Victoria in 1855 regarding the divorce bill before the House of Commons. Norton sought a divorce from her abusive husband, George Norton, whom she had left but could not divorce. He refused to allow her to see or have contact with her sons.

Madam,

On Tuesday, June 13th, of last session, Lord Chancellor Cranworth brought forward a measure for the reform of the Marriage laws of England; which measure was afterwards withdrawn. . . . as one who has grievously suffered, and is still suffering, under the present imperfect state of the law,—I address your Majesty on the subject.

I do not do so in the way of appeal. . . . I know the throne is powerless to redress them. I know those pleasant tales of an earlier and simpler time, when oppressed subjects travelled to the presence of some glorious prince or princess, who instantly set their affairs to rights without reference to law, are quaint old histories, or fairy tales, fit only for the amusement of children.

I connect your Majesty's name with these pages from a different motive; for two reasons: of which one, indeed, is a sequence to the other. First, because I desire to point out the grotesque anomaly which ordains that married women shall be "non-existent" in a country governed by a female Sovereign; and secondly, because, whatever measure for the reform of these statutes may be proposed, it cannot become "the law of the land" without your Majesty's assent and sign manual. In England there is no Salique law. If there were,—if the principles which govern all legislation for the inferior sex in this country, were carried out in their integrity as far as the throne,—your Majesty would be by birth a subject, and Hanover and England would be still under one King.

It is not so. Your Majesty is Queen of England; Head of the Church; Head of the Law; Ruler of millions of men; and the assembled Senate who meet to debate and frame legislative enactments in each succeeding year, *begin* their sessional labours by reverently listening to that clear woman's voice,—rebellion against whose command is treason. . . .

A married woman in England has *no legal existence*: her being is absorbed in that of her husband. Years of separation or desertion cannot alter this position. Unless divorced by special enactment in the House of Lords, the legal fiction holds her to be *"one"* with her husband, even though she may never see or hear of him.

She has no possessions, unless by special settlement; her property is *his* property. . . . An English wife has no legal right even to her clothes or ornaments; her husband may take them and sell them if he pleases, even though they be the gifts of relatives or friends, or bought before marriage.

. . .

An English wife may not leave her husband's house. Not only can he sue her for "restitution of conjugal rights," but he has a right to enter the house of any friend or relation with whom she may take refuge, or who may "harbor her,"—as it is termed,—and carry her away by force, with or without the aid of the police.[1]

II.

The second selection is drawn from a letter written to Queen Victoria in 1868 by one of her ladies-in-waiting and close confidant, Lady Augusta Stanley, while she was on a tour of Ireland. Lady Stanley tried hard to interest the queen in her Irish subjects but did not have much success. She wrote the following extract from the "Donegal Highlands."

The people, who are strong and handsome, are of a less mixed race than in many parts, more purely Celtic. We dined and slept at a most primitive House of "entertainment," where one of Your Majesty's Highland inn chickens would have been a delicacy indeed. . . How much I hope that Your Majesty may some day be able to see some of the peculiar beauties of Irish scenery, as Your Majesty says, and I am certain that Your Majesty in no degree over-estimates the good that would result from it. The people are very sensitive and so alive to anything that honours them and their country and *raises them and it* in their own estimation and in the scale of nations. . . . A lady who lives near Powers Court told me that she had been much struck by the observations of her . . . gardner . . . at the time and after the visit of the Prince and Princess of Wales . . . Many whom he knew well to be filled with the most

1. From Caroline Sheridan Norton, *A Letter to the Queen on Lord Chancellor Cranworth's Marriage and Divorce Bill* (London, 1855).

hostile theories, gradually warmed and warmed, when the theoretical *abstractions* which they thought of at a distance with such bitter feelings, were brought face to face with them in the form of *Persons* whom they could look on an honour, and who were ready to welcome and appreciate them and their Country.—If they could some day find that the Highlands of Donegal or of Connemara or their wild iron bound coasts, which so few visit, were admired and appreciated by Your Majesty and that the poetic legends and traditions of their land and language kindle in Your Majesty the interest I know they would,—it would warm and cheer and fill with enthusiasm, thousands and thousands of hearts.—Your Majesty's experience of Gaelic would make it easier to understand and retain the names than we found it.[2]

III.

The third source, two letters from Queen Victoria to Prime Minister William Gladstone written in May 1870, concerns efforts to enlarge the rights of women and especially to admit women to the medical profession. These were subjects on which the queen and the prime minister held similar opinions, a fairly rare circumstance.

Queen Victoria to Mr. Gladstone, May 6, 1870.
The circumstances respecting the Bill to give women the same position as men with respect to Parliamentary franchise gives her an opportunity to observe that she had for some time past wished to call Mr. Gladstone's attention to the mad & utterly demoralizing movement of the present day to place women in the same

---

2. Extract from the "Donegal Highlands." From The Dean of Windsor and Hector Bolitho, eds., *Later Letters of Lady Augusta Stanley, 1864–1876* (New York, 1929), pp. 95–96.

position as to professions—as *men*;—& amongst others, in the *Medical Line*.

. . . . She is *most* anxious that it shld be known how she not only disapproves but *abhors* the attempts to destroy all propriety & womanly feeling wh will inevitably be the result of what has been proposed. The Queen is a woman herself—& knows what an anomaly her *own* position is:—but that can be reconciled with reason & propriety tho' it is a terrible difficult & trying one. But to tear away all the barriers wh surround a woman, to propose that they shld study with *men*—things sh cld not be named before them—certainly not *in a mixed* audience—wld be to introduce a total disregard of what must be considered as belonging to the rules & principles of morality.

The Queen feels so strongly upon this dangerous & unchristian & unnatural *cry* & movement of "women's rights,"—in wh she knows Mr. Gladstone *agrees*, . . . that she is most anxious that Mr. Gladstone & others shd take some steps to check this alarming danger & to make whatever use they can of her name.

. . . . Let woman be what God intended; a helpmate for a man—but with totally different duties & vocations.

Queen Victoria to Mr. Gladstone, May 8, 1870.
The Queen . . . *feels* the danger as regards the subject . . . to be so *vy serious* that she is determined for the *salvation* of the *young women* of this country—& their *rescue from immorality* to do *every* thing she *can* to put a check to it.—She wishes Mr. Gladstone wld send for & see Sir Wm Jenner [the queen's physician] who can tell him what an *awful* idea this is—of allowing *young girls* & young men to enter the dissecting room together.[3]

3. From Philip Guedalla, ed., *The Queen and Mr. Gladstone, Volume I: 1845–1879* (London, 1933), pp. 227–228.

IV.

The final set of primary sources consists of a series of diary entries made and letters sent to her private secretary, Sir Arthur Bigge, and various cabinet ministers by the queen in late 1899 and 1900 regarding the Boer War.

Journal entry, December 11, 1899

Saw Sir A. Bigge on his return from London, whither he has gone by my desire to see [Commander in Chief of the Forces Garnet] Wolseley and [Secretary for War] Lord Lansdowne, and found the latter depressed and the former much annoyed with the Generals, who he considers have not done what they were advised to do, but have attacked difficult and inaccessible positions, instead of trying to outflank the enemy. Lord Wolseley wanted to know what I thought about it all.

Journal entry, December 14, 1899

The news in the papers is very sad, and there is confirmation of the report of Lord Winchester's and Colonel Downman's deaths, the latter a very nice man, who commanded the Gordon Highlanders . . . Received a list of casualties. The Highlanders lost awfully . . . Feel very low and anxious about the war.

Journal entry, January 11, 1899

After tea saw Lord Rowton [Prime Minister Benjamin Disraeli's private secretary]. Had much to talk with him about the war and our want of preparedness, which has existed for a long time, and which is very culpable.

Letter to Prime Minister Lord Salisbury, January 27, 1900

Am much surprised to see by your telegram and letter that the very serious state of the war was not considered by the Cabinet yesterday. The feeling abroad, except in America and Italy, is so inimical that we ought to take further steps to protect this country, and to raise more troops iof we can. There is not a doubt that the attempted relief of Ladysmith would have succeeded had we had more troops. All Militia must be called out. Red-tapings and useless difficulties must not be regarded at such a very serious moment. The loss of so many valuable lives for nothing is terrible.

Letter to Sir Arthur Bigge, January 27, 1900
The Queen is determined to press any available measure to put us in a safe position, and to put an end to these terrible failures.

Letter to Lord Landsdowne, January 30, 1900
Am glad to hear of the measures determined on. Hope all Cavalry at home will be for ever kept at war footing. Trust that 8th Division will be sent as desired by [Field Marshall] Lord Roberts and as soon as possible. Still think the whole Militia should be embodied. Could not corrugated-iron huts be used instead of tents?

Letter to Lord Lansdowne, January 30, 1900
I am horrified at the terrible list of casualties, twenty-two officers killed and twenty-one wounded. It is quite imperative that Lord Roberts should not move till he has plenty of troops, a really large force. Pray impress this on him. And we must hurry out more troops. You must call out the Militia at once. Would it be possible to warn the young officers not to expose themselves more than is absolutely necessary?

Letter to Colonial Secretary Joseph Chamberlain, February 14, 1900
Please let me know what steps you intend to take to protect the Zulus from being attacked by the Boers. Feel certain you agree with me that we are bound in honour to stand by my native subjects.[4]

4. From Christopher Hibbert, ed., *Queen Victoria in Her Letters and Journals* (New York, 1985), pp. 340–343. Reprinted with permission from David Higham, Literary, Film and TV Agents.

STUDY QUESTIONS

1. How did British society reconcile the fact of a female sovereign ruling over millions of men with the domestic ideology that relegated (middle- and upper-class) women to the home?

2. How did the laws of England comport with the domestic ideology that placed (middle- and upper-class) women on a pedestal as "the angel in the house?"

3. Why was Queen Victoria so indifferent to the Irish people or Ireland as a whole? Why was Lady Stanley so keen to interest her in them?

4. How did Queen Victoria and William Gladstone differ with regard to empire?

5. What were Queen Victoria's attitudes toward her imperial subjects and people of color generally? Did they change over time? If so, why do you think that happened?

6. What were Queen Victoria's concerns about the Boer War?

7. How would you characterize the queen's power and her relationship to and involvement in government?

FURTHER READING

RECOMMENDED PRIMARY SOURCES

There are a great many collections of the letters of Queen Victoria to a variety of people—she wrote constantly and on virtually every subject. See especially:

Benson, Arthur Christopher and Viscount Esher, eds., *The Letters of Queen Victoria: A Selection from Her Majesty's Correspondence Between the Years 1837 and 1861 in Three Volumes*. London: John Murray, 1908.

Buckle, George Earle, ed., *The Letters of Queen Victoria: A Selection from Her Majesty's Correspondence and Journal Between the Years 1862 and 1878 in Two Volumes*. New York: Longmans, Green and Co., 1926.

Buckle, George Earle, ed., *The Letters of Queen Victoria: A Selection from Her Majesty's Correspondence and Journal Between the Years 1886 and 1901 in Three Volumes*. New York: Longmans, Green and Co., 1931.

Queen Victoria's journals are most easily accessed online at http://www.queenvictoriasjournals.org

RECOMMENDED SECONDARY SOURCES

Hundreds of biographies of Queen Victoria exist. The following list contains only some of the ones I found most useful.

Anim-Addo, Joan, "Queen Victoria's Black 'Daughter,'" in Gretchen Holbrook Gerzina, *Black Victorians/Black Victoriana*. New Brunswick, NJ: Rutgers University Press, 2003. A short article about the African girl Victoria was presented with by the king of Dahomey and whom she adopted as her godchild.

Arnstein, Walter L., *Queen Victoria*. Basingstoke, England: Palgrave Macmillan, 2003. A concise and accessible treatment of Queen Victoria's whole life.

Brantlinger, Patrick, *Rule of Darkness: British Literature and Imperialism, 1830–1914*. Ithaca, NY: Cornell University Press, 1988. Discusses British attitudes toward Africans and Africa in the all-important period of nineteenth-century imperialism.

Burton, Antoinette, *Burdens of History: British Feminists, Indian Women, and Imperial Culture, 1865–1915*. Chapel Hill: University of North Carolina Press, 1994. A crucial corrective to all previous works on British feminism. Shows the centrality of putatively debased Indian women to feminist campaigns up to and into World War I.

Clark, Anna, *The Struggle for the Breeches: Gender and the Making of the British Working Class*. Berkeley: University of California Press, 1995. A path-breaking account of the role of gender and sexuality in the formation of the working-class in Britain in the late eighteenth and early nineteenth centuries.

Cohen, Ed, *Talk on the Wilde Side: Toward a Genealogy of a Discourse on Male Sexualities*. New York: Routledge, 1993. A useful account of the development of nineteenth-century norms of masculinity and of British attitudes toward homosexuality as revealed in the press coverage of the trials of Oscar Wilde.

Colley, Linda, *Britons: Forging the Nation, 1707–1837*. New Haven, CT: Yale University Press, 1992. A seminal treatment of the formation of "Britishness" in the eighteenth century.

Erickson, Carolly, *Her Little Majesty. The Life of Queen Victoria*. New York: Simon and Schuster, 2002. Focuses on Queen Victoria's childhood.

Fryer, Peter, *Staying Power. The History of Black People in Britain*. London: Pluto Press, 2010. A crucial work on the presence of blacks in Britain over the past 500 years.

Gillian Gill, *We Two. Victoria and Albert: Rulers, Partners, Rivals*. New York: Ballantine Books, 2010. Treats the years of Victoria's life with her husband, Prince Albert.

Hall, Catherine, *Civilising Subjects. Metropole and Colony in the English Imagination, 1830–1867*. Chicago: University of Chicago Press, 2002. An important examination of the role played by empire in the development of a sense of English national identity.

Hibbert, Christopher, *Queen Victoria, A Personal History*. Cambridge, MA: Da Capo Press, 2000. A thorough and illuminating treatment of the private life of Queen Victoria.

Hibbert, Christopher, ed., *Queen Victoria in Her Letters and Journals*. New York: Viking, 1985. A useful selection.

Homans, Margaret and Adrienne Munich, eds., *Remaking Queen Victoria*. Cambridge: Cambridge University Press, 1997. A series of essays examining the symbolic role played by Queen Victoria in the minds of her subjects. Not an easy read.

Homans, Margaret, *Royal Representations. Queen Victoria and British Culture, 1837–1876*. Chicago: University of Chicago Press, 1998. A scholarly treatment of the interplay between accounts of Queen Victoria and her place in the development of British culture. Not for new students of history.

John, Angela V. and Claire Eustance, eds., *The Men's Share? Masculinities, Male Support and Women's Suffrage in Britain, 1890–1920*. Oxon, England: Routledge, 2014. A collection of essays analyzing the role men played in the women's suffrage campaign in the late nineteenth and early twentieth centuries.

Kent, Susan Kingsley, *Gender and Power in Britain, 1660–1990*. Princeton, NJ: Princeton University Press, 1999. A broad account of the role played by gender in Britain's history since 1660.

Kent, Susan Kingsley, *Sex and Suffrage in Britain, 1860–1914*. Princeton, NJ: Princeton University Press, 1987. An examination of the issues that motivated the women's suffrage campaign in Britain.

Lebow, Richard Ned, *White Britain and Black Ireland: The Influence of Stereotypes on Colonial Policy.* Philadelphia: Institute for the Study of Human Issues, 1976. A helpful look at English attitudes toward Irish people and how they informed Britain's policies toward Ireland.

McDevitt, Patrick, *"May the Best Man Win" Sport, Masculinity, and Nationalism in Great Britain and the Empire, 1880–1935.* Basingstoke, England: Palgrave Macmillan, 2004. An important examination of the role of sport in the consolidation of and resistance to British imperialism.

Meredith, Martin, *Diamonds, Gold and War. The British, the Boers, and the Making of South Africa.* New York: Public Affairs, 2007. A comprehensive and most readable account of the issues that led up to the Anglo-Boer War of 1899–1901.

Metcalf, Thomas, *The New Cambridge History of India, III: Ideologies of the Raj.* Cambridge: Cambridge University Press, 1994. A scholarly but accessible examination of Briton's attitudes toward Indian peoples from the late eighteenth century and how and why they changed over time.

Ó Gráda, Cormac, *Black '47 and Beyond: The Great Irish Famine in History, Economy, and Memory.* Princeton, NJ: Princeton University Press, 1999. A comprehensive account of the Irish famine by one of the subject's foremost experts.

Osborne, Myles and Susan Kingsley Kent, *Africans and Britons in the Age of Empires, 1660–1980.* Oxon, England: Routledge, 2015. A broad account of the interactions between Africans and Britons over 300 years; highlights not only resistance of Africans to empire but their participation in creating and consolidating it as well.

Page, Jesse, *The Black Bishop: Samuel Adjai Crowther.* Westport, CT: Greenwood Press, 1979. The life of Samuel Crowther, who was taken as a slave as a young boy, rescued, and returned to Sierra Leone, where he was educated. He became the first black bishop in West Africa following his ordination in the Church of England.

Pederson, Susan, "Hannah More Meets Simple Simon: Tracts, Chapbooks, and Popular Culture in Late Eighteenth-Century England," *Journal of British Studies* 25, no. 1 (January 1986): 84–113. A brief look at the part played by evangelicals in the formation of the ideology of domesticity and separate spheres for men and women.

Sharpe, Jenny, *Allegories of Empire: The Figure of Woman in the Colonial Text*. Minneapolis: University of Minnesota Press, 1993. A scholarly analysis of the figure of the violated white woman in accounts of British imperial expansion and violence.

Soloway, Richard A., *Demography and Degeneration: Eugenics and the Declining Birth Rate in Twentieth-Century Britain*. Chapel Hill: University of North Carolina Press, 1990. Looks at anxieties about the quality of the British working classes and the British poor in the development of what would become early welfare state policies.

Temperley, Howard, *White Dreams, Black Africa: The Antislavery Expedition to the Niger, 1841–1842*. New Haven, CT: Yale University Press, 1991. A comprehensive and readable account of the people and events who made up the failed Niger Expedition.

Thompson, Dorothy, *Queen Victoria: Gender and Power*. London: Virago, 1990. A focused look at Victoria's role as queen in a period that denied women power and political participation.

Thorne, Susan, " 'The Conversion of Englishmen and the Conversion of the World Inseparable': Missionary Imperialism and the Language of Class in Early Industrial Britain," in Frederick Cooper and Ann Laura Stoler, eds., *Tensions of Empire: Colonial Cultures in a Bourgeois World*. Berkeley: University of California Press, 1997. An important examination of the comparisons made by missionaries between the British working classes and imperial subjects regarded as requiring uplight and civilization. Draws attention to the integration of domestic and imperial histories.

Vallone, Lynne, *Becoming Victoria*. New Haven, CT: Yale University Press, 2001. A helpful look at the influences and practices that went into preparing Victoria to become queen.

Walkowitz, Judith R., *Prostitution and Victorian Society: Women, Class, and the State*. Cambridge: Cambridge University Press, 1980. A path-breaking account of the Ladies' National Association and its campaign to end the Contagious Diseases Acts, laws that compelled women suspected of being prostitutes to submit to physical examination for venereal disease in order to protect the men who utilized their services.

Ward, Margaret, *Unmanageable Revolutionaries: Women and Irish Nationalism*. London: Pluto Press, 1995. A compelling treatment of the part played by Irish women in the crucial years of late nineteenth- and early twentieth-century nationalist politics and their sometime clashes with male political leaders.

Ward, Yvonne, *Censoring Queen Victoria: How Two Gentlemen Edited a Queen and Created an Icon*. London: Oneworld, 2014. An intriguing look at how Viscount Esher and Arthur Benson fashioned a particular picture of and narrative about Queen Victoria as they went about editing her massive volume of letters—see primary sources above.

Wilson, A. N., *Victoria: A Life*. New York: Knopf, 2014. The most recent account of Queen Victoria by the eminent British novelist. Not much that is new here.

Wilson, Kathleen, *The Sense of the People: Politics, Culture and Imperialism in England, 1715–1785*. Cambridge: Cambridge University Press, 1998. Examines the role played by imperial concerns and issues in the development and stimulation of middle-class political participation in the eighteenth century.

NOTES

CHAPTER I

1. Quoted in Mary Poovey, *The Proper Lady and the Woman Writer* (Chicago: University of Chicago Press, 1984), pp. 33, 34.
2. Susan Pederson, "Hannah More Meets Simple Simon: Tracts, Chapbooks, and Popular Culture in Late Eighteenth-Century England," *Journal of British Studies* 25, no. 1 (January 1986): 84–113.
3. Quoted in Anna Clark, *The Struggle for the Breeches: Gender and the Making of the British Working Class* (Berkeley, CA: University of California Press, 1995), p. 155; Iain McCalman, *Radical Underworld: Prophets, Revolutionaries, and Pornographers in London, 1795–1840* (Oxford: Clarendon Press, 1993), p. 167; Clark, *The Struggle for the Breeches*, p. 169.
4. Quoted in McCalman, *Radical Underworld*, p. 172.
5. Quoted in Dror Wahrman, *Imagining the Middle Class: The Political Representations of Class in Britain, c. 1780–1840* (Cambridge: Cambridge University Press, 1995), p. 385; "Wilberforce Correspondence," *Edinburgh Review* 72 (October 1840), p. 65.
6. Quoted in Susan Kingsley Kent, *Gender and Power in Britain, 1640–1990* (London: Routledge, 1999), p. 160.
7. Quoted in Clark, *The Struggle for the Breeches*, pp. 171–72.
8. Ibid., *The Struggle for the Breeches*, p. 170, 171.
9. Ibid., *The Struggle for the Breeches*, p. 173.
10. Quoted in Leonore Davidoff and Catherine Hall, *Family Fortunes: Men and Women of the English Middle Class, 1780–1850* (Chicago: University of Chicago Press, 1987), p. 152.
11. Quoted in Lynne Vallone, *Becoming Victoria* (New Haven, CT: Yale University Press, 2001), pp. 71–72.
12. Quoted in Lynne Vallone, *Becoming Victoria*, p. 65.
13. Quoted in Kent, *Gender and Power in Britain, 1640–1990* (London: Routledge, 1999), pp. 165–166.
14. Wahrman, *Imagining the Middle Class: The Political Representation of Class in Britain, c. 1780–1840* (Cambridge: Cambridge University Press, 1995), ch. 9.
15. Quoted in Thomas Metcalf, *The New Cambridge History of India, III: Ideologies of the Raj* (Cambridge: University of Cambridge Press, 1994), p. 2.
16. R. F. Foster, *Modern Ireland, 1600–1972* (London: Penguin Books, 1989).
17. Quoted in Richard Ned Lebow, *White Britain and Black Ireland: The Influence of Stereotypes on Colonial Policy* (Philadelphia: Institute for the Study of Human Issues, 1976), p. 41.

18. Catherine Hall, "'From Greenland's Icy Mountains . . . to Afric's Golden Sand': Ethnicity, Race and Nation in Mid-Nineteenth-Century England," *Gender and History* 5, no. 2 (1993): 212–230.

19. Quoted in Kent, *Gender and Power in Britain*, p. 207.

20. Catherine Hall, "Missionary Stories: Gender and Ethnicity in England in the 1830s and 1840s," in Lawrence Grossberg et al., *Cultural Studies* (New York: Routledge, 1992), pp. 240–270.

21. Quoted in Hall, "Missionary Stories," p. 258.

22. Ibid., p. 263.

23. Quoted in Patrick Brantlinger, *Rule of Darkness: British Literature and Imperialism, 1830–1914* (Ithaca, NY: Cornell University Press, 1988), pp. 79–81.

24. Quoted in Metcalf, *Ideologies of the Raj*, pp. 33–34.

25. Ibid., p. 34.

CHAPTER 2

1. Quoted in Walter L. Arnstein, *Queen Victoria* (Basingstoke, England: Palgrave Macmillan, 2003), p. 32.

2. Karen Chase and Michael Levenson, "'I never saw a man so frightened': The Young Queen and the Parliamentary Bedchamber," in Margaret Homans and Adrienne Munich, eds., *Remaking Queen Victoria* (Cambridge: Cambridge University Press, 1997), pp. 212–213.

3. Quoted in Gillian Gill, *We Two. Victoria and Albert: Rulers, Partners, Rivals* (New York: Ballantine Books, 2010), pp. 148–149.

4. Letter to Lord Melbourne, May 8, 1839, in Christopher Hibbert, ed., *Queen Victoria in Her Letters and Journals* (New York: Penguin Books, 1985), pp. 48–49.

5. Margaret Homans, *Royal Representations. Queen Victoria and British Culture, 1837–1876* (Chicago: University of Chicago Press, 1998), pp. 14–15.

6. Quoted in Homans, *Royal Representations*, p. 15.

7. Journal entry, April 18, 1839, in Hibbert, ed., *Queen Victoria in Her Letters and Journals*, p. 53.

8. Quoted in Homans, *Royal Representations*, p. 16.

9. Journal entry, July 12, 1839, in Hibbert, ed., *Queen Victoria in Her Letters and Journals*, p. 54.

10. Quoted in Gillian Gill, *We Two*, p. 86.

11. Homans, *Royal Representations*, p. 2.

12. Quoted in Gill, *We Two*, p. 163.

13. Quoted in Susan Kingsley Kent, *Sex and Suffrage in Britain, 1860–1914* (Princeton, NJ: Princeton University Press, 1987), p. 38.

14. Ibid., pp. 38–39.

15. Ibid., pp. 60–61.

16. Journal entries, February 10, 11, and 13, 1840, in Hibbert, ed., *Queen Victoria in Her Letters and Journals*, pp. 64–65.

17. Carolly Erickson, *Her Little Majesty: The Life of Queen Victoria* (New York: Simon and Schuster, 1997), p. 169; quoted in Dorothy Thompson,

Queen Victoria: Gender and Power (London: Virago, 1990), p. 43;
quoted in Erickson, *Her Little Majesty*, p. 169.

18. Ibid., p. 87.

19. Quoted in Gill, *We Two*, p. 165.

20. Ibid., p. 166.

21. Ibid., pp. 167, 343, 169.

22. Quoted in Arnstein, *Queen Victoria*, p. 59.

23. Quoted in Gill, *We Two*, p. 174.

24. Letter to Princess Augusta of Prussia, January 13, 1854, in Hibbert,
ed., *Queen Victoria in Her Letters and Journals*, p. 123.

25. Letter to King Leopold, February 24, 1854, in Hibbert, ed., *Queen
Victoria in Her Letters and Journals*, p. 124.

26. Quoted in Gill, *We Two*, p. 345.

27. Letter to Princess Frederick William, February 13, 1861, in Hibbert,
ed., *Queen Victoria in Her Letters and Journals*, p. 117.

CHAPTER 3

1. Quoted in Arnstein, *Queen Victoria* (Basingstoke, UK: Palgrave
Macmillan, 2003), p. 68.

2. Quoted in Carolly Erickson, *Her Little Majesty: The Life of Queen
Victoria* (New York: Simon and Schuster, 1997), pp. 198–199.

3. Quoted in Joan Huddleston, ed., *Caroline Norton's Defense. English
Laws for Women in the Nineteenth Century* (Chicago: Academy
Chicago, 1982), p. 1.

4. Quoted in Patrick Brantlinger, *Rule of Darkness: British Literature
and Imperialism, 1830–1914* (Ithaca, NY: Cornell University Press,
1988), p. 32.

5. Quoted in Howard Temperley, *White Dreams, Black Africa: The Antislavery Expedition to the Niger, 1841–1842* (New Haven, CT: Yale
University Press, 1991), pp. 157, 162.

6. Quoted in Brantlinger, *Rule of Darkness*, p. 178.

7. In what follows, see Eugene R. August, ed., *Thomas Carlyle, "The
Nigger Question." John Stuart Mill, "The Negro Question"* (New York:
Appleton-Century-Crofts, 1971).

8. For this and previous quotes see Eugene r. August, ed., *Thomas
Carlyle, The Nigger Question; John Stuart Mill, The Negro Question* (New York: Appleton-Century-Crofts, 1971), pp. 1–37.

9. Quoted in Walter L. Arnstein, *Queen Victoria*, pp. 141, 181.

10. Quoted in http://www.blackpast.org/aah/bonetta-sarah-forbes-
1843–1880#sthash.j1bqzUaO.dpufhttp://www.blackpast.org/aah/
bonetta-sarah-forbes-1843–1880#sthash.j1bqzUaO.dpuf. Frederick
F. Forbes, *Dahomey and the Dahomians: Being the Journals of Two
Missions to the King of Dahomey and Residence at His Capital in the
Years 1849 and 1850* (London: Longman, Brown, Green & Longman,
1851), p. 193.

11. Quoted in Jesse Page, *The Black Bishop: Samuel Adjai Crowther*
(Westport, CT: Greenwood Press, 1979), p. 104.

12. Joan Anim-Addo, "Queen Victoria's Black 'Daughter,'" in Gretchen Holbrook Gerzina, *Black Victorians/Black Victoriana* (New Brunswick, NJ: Rutgers University Press, 2003).

13. Quoted in Carlyle, *"The Nigger Question."*

14. Quoted in Arnstein, *Queen Victoria*, p. 75.

15. Quoted in Richard Ned Lebow, *White Britain and Black Ireland. The Influence of Stereotypes on Colonial Policy* (Philadelphia: Institute for the Study of Human Issues, 1976), pp. 39–40.

16. Ibid., p. 57.

17. Ibid., pp. 62–63, 67.

18. Quoted in Arnstein, *Queen Victoria*, p. 79.

19. Ibid., p. 80.

20. Ibid., p. 80.

21. Quoted in Thomas Metcalf, *Ideologies of the Raj* (Cambridge: Cambridge University Press, 1994), p. 58.

22. Quoted in Christopher Hibbert, *Queen Victoria, A Personal History* (Cambridge, MA: Da Capo Press, 2000), p. 251.

23. Letter to Lady Canning, October 22, 1857, in Hibbert, ed., *Queen Victoria in Her Letters and Journals* (New York: Penguin Books, 1985), pp. 137–138.

24. Quoted in Jenny Sharpe, *Allegories of Empire: The Figure of Woman in the Colonial Text* (Minneapolis: University of Minnesota Press, 1993), ch. 3.

25. George Otto Trevelyan, *Cawnpore* (New Delhi, 1992; originally published 1865), p. 18; quoted in Brantlinger, *Rule of Darkness*, p. 209.

26. Quoted in Hibbert, *Queen Victoria*, p. 250.

27. Quoted in Brantlinger, *Rule of Darkness*, p. 209.

28. Trevelyan, *Cawnpore*, p. 75.

29. See James Belich, *Making Peoples: A History of the New Zealanders* (Honolulu: University of Hawai'i Press, 2001), pp. 193–97.

30. Quoted in James Morris, *Heaven's Command: An Imperial Progress* (New York: Harvest, 1973), p. 54.

31. Quoted in Philip Curtin, Steven Feierman, Leonard Thompson, and Jan Vansina, *African History* (Boston: Little, Brown and Company, 1978), p. 323.

32. Ibid., p. 325.

CHAPTER 4

1. Letter to the Crown Princess of Prussia, December 18, 1861, Christopher Hibbert, ed., *Queen Victoria in Her Letters and Journals* (New York: Penguin Books, 1985), pp. 157, 159.

2. Quoted in Dorothy Thompson, *Queen Victoria, Gender and Power* (London: Virago, 1990), p. 59.

3. Quoted in Gillian Gill, *We Two. Victoria and Albert: Rulers, Partners, Rivals* (New York: Ballantine Books, 2010), pp. 375–376.

4. Letter to Lord Russell, January 22, 1866, in Hibbert, ed., *Queen Victoria in Her Letters and Journals*, p. 193.

5. Quoted in Arnstein, *Queen Victoria*, p. 123.

6. Gill, *We Two*, p. 379.

7. Letter to the Crown Princess of Prussia, April 5, 1865, in Hibbert, ed., *Queen Victoria in Her Letters and Journals*, p. 188.

8. Letter to Lord Charles FitzRoy, June 26, 1867, in Hibbert, ed., *Queen Victoria in Her Letters and Journals*, p. 199.

9. Quoted in Thompson, *Queen Victoria*, p. 86.

10. Quoted in Thompson, *Queen Victoria*, pp. 64, 76, 68; Hibbert, *Queen Victoria*, pp. 326–327.

11. Letter to the Crown Princess of Prussia, April 8, 1883, in Hibbert, ed., *Queen Victoria in Her Letters and Journals*, p. 281.

12. Quoted in Thompson, *Queen Victoria*, p. 67.

13. Ibid., *Queen Victoria*, p. 77.

14. Ibid., p. 78.

15. Quoted in Christopher Hibbert, *Queen Victoria, A Personal History*, (Cambridge, MA: Da Capo Press, 2000).

16. Ibid., p. 310.

17. Letter to Theodore Martin, May 14, 1868, in Hibbert, ed., *Queen Victoria in Her Letters and Journals*, p. 205.

18. Quoted in Thompson, *Queen Victoria*, p. 107.

19. Ibid., p. 115.

20. Quoted in Kent, *Sex and Suffrage*, p. 187.

21. Ibid., p. 190.

22. Ibid., pp. 190–191.

23. Ibid., pp. 190–191.

24. Ibid., pp. 192–193.

25. Ibid., pp. 193–194.

26. Catherine Hall, "Imperial Man: Edward Eyre in Australasia and the West Indies," in Bill Schwartz, ed., *The Expansion of England: Race, Ethnicity and Cultural History* (London: Routledge, 1996), p. 283.

27. Ibid., pp. 162, 160; Hall, *White, Male and Middle Class*, pp. 284–285.

28. Letter to the Crown Princess of Prussia, October 14, 1867, in Hibbert, ed., *Queen Victoria in Her Letters and Journals*, p. 200.

29. Quoted in Lebow, *White Britain*, p. 40.

30. Quoted in Morris, *Heaven's Command*, p. 342.

31. Ibid., p. 343.

32. Ibid., p. 345.

33. Ibid., p. 348.

34. For the discussion of the Reform Act of 1867, I rely upon Anna Clark, "Gender, Class, and the Nation: Franchise Reform in England, 1832–1928," in James Vernon, ed., *Re-Reading the Constitution: New Narratives in the Political History of England's Long Nineteenth Century* (Cambridge: Cambridge University Press, 1996).

35. Quoted in Susan Thorne, "'The Conversion of Englishmen and the Conversion of the World Inseparable': Missionary Imperialism and the Language of Class in Early Industrial Britain," in Frederick Cooper and Ann Laura Stoler, eds., *Tensions of Empire: Colonial*

Cultures in a Bourgeois World (Berkeley: University of California Press, 1997), p. 249.

CHAPTER 5

1. Quoted in James Morris, *Heaven's Command* (London: Farber, 1973), p. 382.
2. Quoted in Walter Arnstein, *Queen Victoria* (Basingstoke: Palgrave Macmillan, 2003), p. 140.
3. Quoted in James Morris, *Heaven's Command*, (London: Farber, 1973), p. 420.
4. Journal entry, November 24, 1875, in Christopher Hibbert, ed., *Queen Victoria in Her Letters and Journals* (New York: Viking, 1985), p. 241.
5. Journal entries, February 26 and March, 14, 1876, in Hibbert, ed., *Queen Victoria in Her Letters and Journals*, p. 242.
6. "Proclamation of the Empire in India," *Illustrated London News*, January 6, 1877, p. 18.
7. Quoted in Saul David, *Zulu: The True Story*. BBC online, February 17, 2012. http://www.bbc.co.uk/history/british/victorians/zulu_01.shtml
8. Journal entry, February 28, 1881; letter to Lord Kimberley, colonial secretary, March 9, 1881; journal entry May 29, 1881, in Hibbert, ed., *Queen Victoria in Her Letters and Journals*, pp. 268, 270.
9. Letter to Gladstone, February 9, 1883, in Hibbert, ed., *Queen Victoria in Her Letters and Journals*, p. 284.
10. Letter to Hartington, March 25, 1884, in Hibbert, ed., *Queen Victoria in Her Letters and Journals*, pp. 285.
11. Letter to Ponsonby, May 17, 1884, in Hibbert, ed., *Queen Victoria in Her Letters and Journals*, p. 286.
12. Quoted in Morris, *Heaven's Command*, p. 510.
13. Journal entry, February 5, 1885, in Hibbert, ed., *Queen Victoria in Her Letters and Journals*, pp. 289.
14. Letter to Ponsonby, February 17, 1885, ibid., p. 290.
15. Letter to Lord Wolseley, March 31, 1885, ibid., p. 291.
16. Letter to Lord Hartington, May 17, 1885, ibid., p. 292.
17. Letter to Lord Hartington, December 12, 1880, ibid., p. 265.
18. Letter to W. E. Forster, December 25, 1880, ibid. p. 266.
19. Letter to Lord Hartington, January 16, 1881, ibid., p. 267.
20. Quoted in Margaret Ward, *Unmanageable Revolutionaries: Women and Irish Nationalism* (London: Pluto Press, 1995), p. 13.
21. Letter to Gladstone, December 31, 1881, in Hibbert, ed., *Queen Victoria in Her Letters and Journals*, p. 271.
22. Ward, *Unmanageable Revolutionaries*, p. 30.
23. Quoted in Ward, *Unmanageable Revolutionaries*, pp. 28–29.
24. Letter to Lord Granville, May 7, 1882, in Hibbert, ed., *Queen Victoria in Her Letters and Journals*, p. 273.
25. Letter to Gladstone, May 6, 1886, ibid., p. 298.

26. This discussion draws from Patrick F. McDevitt, "Muscular Catholicism: Nationalism, Masculinity and Gaelic Team Sports, 1884–1916," *Gender and History* 9, no. 2 (1997): 262–284.

27. Ibid., pp. 262–284.

28. Susan Kingsley Kent, *Sex and Suffrage in Britain, 1860–1914* (Princeton: Princeton University Press, 1987), ch. 7.

29. Judith R. Walkowitz, *Prostitution and Victorian Society: Women, Class, and the State* (Cambridge: Cambridge University Press, 1980); and Kent, *Sex and Suffrage in Britain*, ch. 2.

30. Quoted in Kent, *Sex and Suffrage in Britain*, p. 66.

31. Ibid., p. 69.

32. Ibid., p. 75.

33. Ibid., p. 75.

34. Ibid., pp. 77–78.

CHAPTER 6

1. Quoted in Susan Kingsley Kent, *Sex and Suffrage in Britain, 1860–1914* (Princeton, NJ: Princeton University Press, 1987), p. 80.

2. Ibid., p. 80.

3. Ibid., p. 81.

4. Ibid., p. 83.

5. Ibid., p. 51.

6. Ed Cohen, *Talk on the Wilde Side: Toward a Genealogy of a Discourse on Male Sexualities* (New York: Routledge, 1993), p. 136; Angela V. John and Claire Eustance, eds., *The Men's Share? Masculinities, Male Support and Women's Suffrage in Britain, 1890—1920* (London: Routledge, 1997), p. 7.

7. Quoted in Kent, *Sex and Suffrage in Britain*, p. 84.

8. Ibid., pp. 102, 103.

9. Ibid., p. 88.

10. Ibid., p. 89.

11. Ibid., p. 92.

12. Ibid., p. 93.

13. Ibid., p. 95.

14. Ibid., p. 105.

15. Ibid., p. 112.

16. Quoted in James Morris, *Heaven's Command* (London: Faber, 1973), p. 522.

17. Quoted in Morris, *Heaven's Command*, p. 527.

18. Telegram to German Emperor, January 5, 1896, in Hibbert, ed., *Queen Victoria in Her Letters and Journals*, p. 332.

19. Richard A. Soloway, *Demography and Degeneration: Eugenics and the Declining Birth Rate in Twentieth-Century Britain* (Chapel Hill, NC: University of North Carolina Press, 1990), p. 39.

20. Quoted in Bernard Porter, *The Lion's Share: A Short History of British Imperialism, 1850—1983* (London: Pearson, 1975), p. 130.

21. Quoted in Porter, *The Lion's Share*, p. 129.

22. Quoted in Susan Kingsley Kent, *Gender and Power in Britain, 1640–1990* (London: Routledge, 1999), p. 238.

23. Quoted in Walter Arnstein, *Queen Victoria* (Basingstoke: Palgrave Macmillan, 2003), p. 188.

24. Quoted in James Morris, *Farewell the Trumpets: An Imperial Retreat* (London: Faber, 1979), p. 66.

25. Quoted in Arnstein, *Queen Victoria*, p. 191.

26. Journal entry, October 19, 1899, in Hibbert, ed., *Queen Victoria in Her Letters and Journals*, p. 339.

27. Letter to Lord Lansdowne, October 22, 1899; journal entry, December 11, 1899, in Hibbert, ed., *Queen Victoria in Her Letters and Journals*, p. 340.

28. Quoted in Hibbert, *Queen Victoria*, p. 459.

29. Journal entry, January 11, 1900; letter to Salisbury, January 27, 1900; letter to A. Bigge, January 30, 1900, in Hibbert, ed., *Queen Victoria in Her Letters and Journals*, p. 341.

30. Quoted in Arnstein, *Queen Victoria*, p. 192.

31. Ibid., p. 192.

CHAPTER 7

1. Piers Brendon, *The Decline and Fall of the British Empire, 1781–1997* (New York: Vintage, 2007), p. 231.

2. The classic account of this phenomenon will be found in Anna Davin, "Imperialism and Motherhood," in Frederick Cooper and Ann Laura Stoler, eds., *Tensions of Empire: Colonial Cultures in a Bourgeois World* (Berkeley: University of California Press, 1997).

3. Davin, "Imperialism and Motherhood," pp. 93–94.

4. Ibid., p. 94.

5. This account is based on Ellen Ross, *Love and Toil: Motherhood in Outcast London, 1870–1918* (New York: Oxford University Press, 1993).

6. Ibid., p. 197.

CREDITS

INDEX

Act of Union (1801), 78

Acton, William, 49, 50–51

Adelaide of Saxe-Meningen, Royal Consort of William IV, 14

adultery, laws concerning, 67

Africa; imperialist scramble for, 2, 128–37, *130*, 132*f*, 133*f*; South African Company, 161–62; South African War, 169–76, *172*; Union of South Africa, 174

Afrikaners (Boers), 88–92, 128–31, 132*f*; Jameson Raid on, 162–64; South African War, 169–76, *172*

Alan Quatermain (Haggard), 167

Albert "Bertie," Prince of Wales (son), 8, 53, 72, 80, 94; racial thinking instilled in, 74; stirs pro-royalty sentiment, 104–5

Albert of Saxe-Coburg and Gotha, Prince Consort (husband), 1, 20; accused of treason, 59–60; as co-ruler, 56–57, 63; family relations, 53–55, *55*; mourning at death of, 93–96, *95*; Niger Anti-Slavery debacle, 68–69; prudery of, 57–58; wedding and early married life of, 45, 45–48, 51–52

Alexandra College, Dublin, 106

Alfred, Duke of Saxe-Coburg and Gotha (son), 53

Algeria, 132*f*, 133*f*

Alice, Grand Duchess of Hesse (daughter), 53

American colonies, 27. *See also* United States

"angel in the house" ideology, 146, 148, 150–51

Anglo-Egyptian Sudan, 133*f*

Angola, 133*f*

aristocracy, 13–14, 24, 57–58, 62

Arthur William Patrick Albert, Prince (son), 54, 80, 133

"Article on Government" (Mill, James), 21

Artisans, Mechanics, and Labouring Classes of Manchester, 11

Asquith, Herbert Henry, 179

assassination attempt, 79

Australia, 27, 88

Bagehot, Walter, 2

Bahadur Shah Zafar II, Emperor of Hindustan, 81

Balfour, A. J., 171, 175–76

Balmoral castle, 61–62, 94–98, *97*, 100–102

Basutoland, 133*f*

Basuto people, 89

Bateson, Thomas, 121

Beale, Dorothea, 66

Beatrice, Princess (daughter), 54

Becker, Lydia, 106
bedchamber crisis, 42–43
Belfast, 106
Belgium, 3, 17, 131, 132*f*, 133*f*
Benbow, William, 10, 13
Bentinck, Lord William, 32, 34
Bertie. *See* Albert "Bertie," Prince of Wales
Besant, Annie, 160
Bibighar, India, 84–85
Bigge, Arthur, 186–88, 189
Bill of Pains and Penalties, 9, 13
Black Dwarf, 9, 11, 12
Black Week (December,1899), 171
Bodichon, Barbara Leigh Smith, 65–66, 106
Boer War, 169–76, *172. See also* Afrikaners; Bigge on, 186–88, 189
Bonetta, Sarah Forbes (goddaughter), *73*, 73–74
Boucherett, Jessie, 66, 106
bourgeois morality, 62
Bradlaugh, Charles, 104, 160
A Brief Summary in Plain Language of the Most Important Laws Concerning Women (Bodichon), 66
Bright, John, 105, 121
British Columbia, 27
British Empire; in 1837, 23*f*; in 1900, 168*f*; concentration camps with women and children, *172*, 173; Disraeli policies, 122, 123–32, *124*, *127*; expansion in Africa, 2,

128–37, 132*f*, 133*f*; fitness to rule, 38–40; Gladstone policies, 131–42; liberal versus conservative views regarding, 50, 75–77, 80–82; mother of, 105, *130*, 167; slavery in, 28–29, 67–72, 90; as source of wealth, power, and virtue, 27, 165–66; South African War, 169–76, *172*
Brougham, Lord, 42
Brown, John, 61–62, 96–99, *97*, 101–4
Buckingham Palace, 36
Buller, Charles, 22
Burke, Thomas, 141
Burma, 27
Burundi, 133*f*
Buss, Mary Frances, 66
Butler, Josephine, 145–49
Buxton, Thomas Fowell, 68
Byrne, Harriet, 140

Caird, Mona, 154–55, 157–59
Cameroon, 133*f*
Campbell, John, 120
Canada, 27, 115–19
Candler, John, 30
Canning, Lady, 83
Canterbury, Archbishop of, 19, 36
Cape Colony, 91–92, 128, 132*f*, 133*f*, 163
Cape of Good Hope, 88–89, 131
Caribbean, 88
Carlyle, Thomas, 69–72, 74–75, 80, 112–13

Caroline of Brunswick, Royal
    Consort of George IV, 3,
    9–15
Carpenter, Edward, 153
Cavendish, Frederick, 141
Cawnpore (Trevelyan, G.), 85
Cetshwayo, King of Zulus,
    128–29
Chamberlain, Joseph, 36, 161,
    163, 188
Charlotte Augusta, Princess
    of Wales, 3
Chartism, 38, 121
*Cheap Repository of Moral and
    Religious Tracts* (More), 5, 12
Chelmsford, Lord, 129–30
Cheltenham Ladies' College,
    66, 74
Children's Act (1908), 177
chloroform, 1, 54
Christianity; evangelical, 4–6,
    14, 24, 28; Irish Catholics,
    24–25, 26, 77, 114–15,
    143–44; missionaries, 31–32,
    73–74, 90; muscular, 87–88,
    89–92
Churchill, Winston, 169
Church of England, 39
Church of Ireland, 39
citizenship, conference of,
    20–21
civilization, women as measure
    of, 15, 30–32, 33, 86
Clapham sect, 4
Clarendon, Lord, 102
Cobbett, Anne, 13
Cobbett, William, 13
Comoro Islands, 133*f*
concentration camps, *172*, 173

Congo, 133*f*
Conroy, John, 17–19, *18*, 44
constitutional monarchy, 39
Contagious Diseases Acts
    (1864, 1866), 144–50
contraception, 152, 160
Corn Laws (1815), 8, 70, 75–76
coverture, 152–53. *See also*
    women rights/suffrage
Cranworth, Lord Chancellor,
    182–84
Crawford, George, 78–79
Crimean War, 60–61
Criminal Law Amendment Act
    (1885), 154
Croke, Archbishop, 144
Crowder, Samuel, 74
Cruikshank, George, 78
Cumberland, Duke of, 17
Curzon, Lord, 161
Cusack, Michael, 144
Custody Act (1839), 64–65

Dahomey, Africa, 73
dandies, 8–9
Darwin, Charles, 80, 87–88,
    165–66
Daughters of Danaus
    (Caird), 155
Davies, Emily, 106
Davitt, Michael, 137–41
Davys, George, 19
Dawn Island (Martineau), 68
Delhi, 81, 127, *127*
diamonds; Diamond Jubilee of
    1897, 160, 167; as incentive
    for political control, 128
Dickens, Charles, 69, 80, 112
diktats (dictates), 59

Dingane, King of Zulus, 90–91
Disraeli, Benjamin, 78, 99, 107; new imperialism of, 122, 123–32, *124*, *127*
divorce, 9–15, 66–67; Norton, C., letter about, 182–84
Dixie, Florence, 160
Drysdale, George, 49–50
Dublin, 79–80, 106–7, 141
Durham, Jack, 89
Durham Report, 91–92

Earl of Dublin, 80
East India Company, 32, 83
Edward, Prince, Duke of Kent and Strathearn. *See* George IV
Edward VII, King. *See also* Albert "Bertie," Prince of Wales; removal of evidence by, 101–2; as symbol of upcoming changes, 175
Egypt, *124*, 124–28, 132*f*, 133*f*, 134
The Elements of Social Science (Drysdale), 49–50
Ellis, Henry Havelock, 153
Elmy, Elizabeth Wolstenholme, 159–60
Empress of India, 126–27, *127*
"Enfranchisement of Women" (Mill, H. T.), 107–8
English Laws for Women (Norton, C.), 65
Eritrea, 133*f*
"Essay on Robert Clive" (Macaulay), 32
Ethiopia, 132*f*, 133*f*
Eyre, Edward, 111–13

Fair Play, or Who Are the Adulterers, Slanderers and Demoralizers? (Benbow), 10
"family of man" concept, 29–30
Fawcett, Millicent, 160
Fenians, 80, 113–15, 137, 143
First Council, 37
First Love and Last Love: A Tale of the Indian Mutiny (Grant), 85
Forbes, Frederick, 73
France, 104, 131, 132*f*, 133*f*
free trade, 20, 70
French Congo, 133*f*
French Somaliland, 133*f*
French West Africa, 133*f*
Frere, Bartle, 128
Functions and Disorders of the Reproductive Organs (Acton), 49, 50–51

Gaelic Athletic Association, 143–44
Gaelic renaissance (1880–1910), 142–44
Gambia, 132*f*, 133*f*, 162
Garrett, Elizabeth, 106, 152
gender roles. *See also* language of gender and sexuality; changing, impacting social behavior, 6–9, 87; evangelical ideals of, 5–6, 14; female regnancy as paradox in, 40–41, 189; Gaelic renaissance and, 142–44; manliness of hunting, 167; marital relations reflecting, 48–49; Queen Caroline affair impacting, 9–15; separate

sphere ideology and, 6–7, 12–15, 29–30; wearing apparel and, 6

George III, King (grandfather), 3–4

George IV, King, 3–4, 9–15, 16, 40

Germany, 131, 132*f*, 133*f*

Ghillies Balls, 100

Girton College, Cambridge, 105

Gladstone, William, 121–22, 124–26, 131–42; letters to, 185–86, 189

Glencoe, 171

"Glorious Deeds of Women" (Benbow), 13

Glorious Revolution (1688), 39

gold, as incentive for political control, 128, 169–70

Gold Coast, 27, 133*f*, 162

Goldie, George, 161

Gordon, Charles, 134–37

Gordon, George, 111

Government of India Act (1858), 83

Grand, Sarah, 154–55

Grant, James, 85

Grenville, Lord Charles, 56

Grey, Charles, 102

Guinea, 132*f*, 133*f*

Haggard, H. Rider, 166–67

Hartington, Lord, 138

Haslam, Anna, 106–7

Hastings, Lady Flora, 44

Helena, Princess (daughter), 53

Henry VIII, King, 24

homosexuality, 154

Hong Kong, 27

Hudson's Bay Company, 115

Hume, Hamilton, 113

Hume-Rothery, Mary, 147

hunting, manliness of, 167

India; British control in, 8–9, 23*f*, 24, 27, 32–33, 168*f*; characterized by language of gender and sexuality, 8–9, 32–33, 83–85; characterizing women of, 34; as either Colony or Conquest, 81–83; Empress of, 126–27, *127*; Indian Mutiny in, 2, 80–82, *81*; new imperialism in, 122, 123–32, *124*, *127*

industrialization, 88–89, 164–67; enfranchisement of working classes, 39; language of political economy, 156–60; separate sphere ideology and, 6–7, 12–15, 29–30, 38–41, 107–8, 145–50

infant mortality rate, 164–65

infant welfare movement, 177–78

Irish people; Carlyle on, 74–75; Catholic, 24–25, 26, 77, 114–15, 143–44; characterized by language of gender and sexuality, 78, 113–15; Fenians, 80, 113–15, 137–43; home rule for, 2, 78–79, 142, 179–80; potato famine of, 75, 75–77; Stanley letter about, 184–85, 189

Irish Republican Brotherhood, 113

Irish Women Suffrage and Local Government Association, Dublin, 106–7
Isandhlwana, Zululand, 129
Italian Somaliland, 133f
Italy, 131, 132f, 133f

Jamaica, 31–32, 69–72
Jamaica Bill, 42–43
James II, King, 25
Jameson, Leander Starr, 163–64
Jameson Raid, 162–64
Japan, 178
Jenner, William, 102–3

Kensington Palace, 36
Kensington system, 17–19
Kenya, 162
Khartoum, Sudan, 135–37
khedive of Egypt, 124, 125
Khoikhoi people, 89–90
Kilmainham Treaty, 141
Kimberley diamond mines, 162
Kingsley, Charles, 112
King Solomon's Mine (Haggard), 167
Kitchener, General, 162
Knibb, William, 30, 31
Kruger, Paul, 163–64

Ladies Land League, 139–41
Ladies National Association for the Repeal of the Contagious Diseases Acts (LNA), 145–50
Lagos, 132f
Lamb, William. See Melbourne, Lord
Land League, 137–41
Langham Place, 66, 105, 106

language of gender and sexuality. See also gender roles; racial hatred; applied to aristocracy, 8–9, 32–33; class defined in, 121; foreigners characterized by, 26; Indians characterized by, 8–9, 32–33, 83–85; Irish characterized by, 78, 113–15; people of color characterized by, 71–72, 112–13
language of political economy, feminist use of, 156–60
Lansdowne, Lord, 187, 188
Lawrence, George, 86
Lehzen, Baroness Louise (governess), 19–20, 56
Leopold, Prince, Duke of Albany (son), 54
Leopold I, King of Belgians, 3, 17
lesbianism, 154
Leslie, Marion, 158
A Letter to the Queen on Lord Cranworth's Marriage and Divorce Bill (Norton, C.), 67
liberal ideology, 20–21; contradictions in implementing, 26–28; female regnancy as paradox for, 40–41, 189; Indian Mutiny drowns out, 2, 80–82, 81; Irish famine and, 75, 75–77; on racial differences, 80; on right to possess, 22–24; upper class interests and, 24; welfare programs versus, 177–79
Liberia, 132f, 133f
Libya, 133f
Linton, Eliza Lynn, 156
Lloyd George, David, 179

LNA. *See* Ladies National Association for the Repeal of the Contagious Diseases Acts
London Missionary Society, 90
London School of Medicine for Women, 106. *See also* women rights/suffrage
Louise, Princess (daughter), 53
Lowe, Robert, 120
Luddites, 8
Lynch, Hannah, 140
Lytton, Lord, 127

Macaulay, Thomas Babington, 22, 32
MacDougall, William, 116–19
Madagascar, 132*f*, 133*f*
Mahdi, the, 134
Manitoba, 115–19
Manitoba Act (1870), 118
Maori people, 88
Married Women's Property Acts (1870, 1882, 1893), 65
Martin, Anna, 178
Martin, Theodore, 103
Martineau, Harriet, 68
Matabele people, 89
Matrimonial Causes Act (1857), 67
Maurice, Frederick, 176
Maurice Dering (Lawrence), 86
Maximilian I, Emperor of Mexico, 99
McIlquham, Harriet, 158–59
Melbourne, Lord (William Lamb), 10–11, 37–38, *38*, 42–43
meritocracy, 20
Métis people, 115–19

middle classes. *See also* separate sphere ideology; abolitionist position among, 29; alliance with radicals, 8, 14, 20, 38; bourgeois morality, 62; Buller on intelligence of, 22; conformance to, 169; monarchy popular among, 57–58; political and social sway of, 4–7; on Queen Caroline plight, 13; in reform movement, 8; Society for Promoting the Employment of Women, 66; women as models of submission, 5–6
Mill, Harriet Taylor, 107–9
Mill, James, 21
Mill, John Stuart, 28, 80, 107–9, 111–12
Milner, Lord, 161
"Minute on Education" (Macaulay), 33
missionaries, 31–32, 73–74, 90
monarchy; as mother figure, 105, *130*, 167; popularity among middle classes, 57–58; pro-royalty sentiment, 104–5; state power of, 39–40, 189; strengthened by Queen Caroline affair, 15
Morant Bay, Jamaica, 111–13
More, Hannah, 4–6, 12, 19, 24
Morocco, 133*f*
Mother of British Empire, 105, *130*, 167
Mozambique, 133*f*
"Murder of George Crawford and his Granddaughter" (Cruikshank), 78–79

Nana Sahib, 84–85
Napier, George, 90
Natal, 27, 91–92, 128, 132*f*
National Society for Women's
    Suffrage, 109
Native Americans, 26
native races, 72, 88. *See also*
    people of color
New Brunswick, 115
Newnham College, Oxford,
    105–6
New South Wales, 88
New Town Type, 176
New Woman authors, 153–55
New Zealand, 27, 88
Niger Anti-Slavery Expedition,
    68–69
"The Niger Expedition"
    (Dickens), 69
Nigeria, 27, 162
"The Nigger Question"
    (Carlyle), 70–71
North America, 26–27
North of London Collegiate
    School for Ladies, 66
Northumberland, Duchess of, 17
Norton, Caroline, 64–65, 67,
    182–84
Norton, George, 65
Notification of Births Act
    (1907), 177
Nova Scotia, 115

"Occasional Discourse on
    the Nigger Question"
    (Carlyle), 70
O'Connell, Daniel, 78
"Ode to George the Fourth and
    Caroline his wife," 14

old corruption, 8, 10, 20
O'Leary, Ellen, 140
Ontario, 115
Orange, William of, 25
Orange Free State, 128, 132*f*
O'Shea, Kitty, 142
Ottoman Empire, 132*f*
Oudh, India, 27, 81

Paine, Thomas, 7
Palmerston, Lady, 10
Paris Commune, 104
Parkes, Bessie Raynor, 65
Parliament Act (1911), 179–80
Parnell, Anna, 139
Parnell, Charles, 138–43
Parnell, Delia, 139
Parnell, Fanny, 139
passionless woman, 153–54
paternalism, white, 29–30
patronage, 20
Pax Britannica, 169
Peel, Robert, 43–44, 75–76
pensions, old-age, 179
people of color; changing atti-
    tudes toward, 72, 189; char-
    acterized by language of
    gender and sexuality, 71–72,
    112–13; colonies of whites
    versus colonies of, 27,
    87–89; derision and degra-
    dation of, 69–71; empire as
    despotic rule over, 123–24;
    enslavement of, 28–29,
    67–72, 90; paternalism
    toward, 29–30; social Dar-
    winism applied to, 80,
    87–88, 165–66
People's Budget, 179

Phillip, John, 90
Phillippo, James, 29, 30–31
Ponsonby, Henry, 101, 135
poor rates, 7–8
poor relief, 22
Port Natal, 90
Portugal, 132*f*, 133*f*
Power, Jenny, 140
prime minister, role of, 39
prostitution, in England, 144–50
prudery, 57–58, 62
Prussia, 104
Punjab, 27, 81

Quebec, 115
Queen Caroline affair, 9–15
Queen's College, 66

race degeneration, 176
racial hatred, 69–72. *See also* language of gender and sexuality; disavowed, 74, 86; social Darwinism and, 80, 87–88, 165–66
radicals; language of gender and sexuality applied to aristocracy, 8–9, 32–33; middle class alliance with, 8, 14, 20, 38; Queen Caroline affair as opportunity for, 9–15
rape, marital, 157–59
Red River colony, 115–19
Reform Acts (1832, 1867), 20, 32, 107
Regina v. Clarence (1888), 158–59
Reid, James, 101
Representation of the People Act (1918), 181

responsible government, 88, 91–92
Reynolds, Hannah, 140
Rhodes, Cecil, 161, *163*
Rhodesia, 133*f*, 162
Riel, Louis, 116–19
Roberts, Lord, 188
Rosebery, Lord, 161, 165
Rowton, Lord, 187
Roy, Ram Mohan, 34
Royal Marriage Act (1772), 3–4
Royal Niger Company, 161–62
Royal Titles Bill, 126
Russell, Earl, 120–21
Russell, John, 89, 95
Russia, 59–61, 178
Rwanda, 133*f*

Salisbury, Lord, 187–88
San people, 89
sati (widow burning), 34
Schreiner, Olive, 156
Scotland, 23*f*, 24; Balmoral castle, 61–62, 94–98, *97*, 100–102
Scott, Thomas, 118–19
Senegal, 133*f*
separate sphere ideology; female regnancy as paradox for, 40–41, 189; LNA versus, 145–50; refutation of, 107–8; upper class adoption of, 6–7, 12–15, 29–30; among working classes, 12–13, 38–39
Shore, Arabella, 110–11
Sierra Leone, 27, 73–74, 132*f*, 133*f*, 162
Sikhs, 81

slavery, 28–29, 67–72, 90

Smith, Thomas, 25

Snow, John, 54

social Darwinism, 80, 87–88, 165–66

Society for Promoting the Employment of Women, 66

Somaliland, 133*f*, 162

South Africa, 27, 89–92, 128–32

South African Company, 161–62

South African Republic, 132*f*

South African War (1899–1901), 169–76, *172*

South West Africa, 133*f*

Stanley, Lady Augusta, 184–85

Stockmar, Baron, 53

The Story of an African Farm (Schreiner), 156

Stritch, Claire, 140

The Subjection of Women (Mill, J. S.), 107–8

Sudan, 133*f*, 134–37

Suez Canal, *124*, 124–28

suffrage. *See also* women rights/ suffrage; in Ireland, 106–7; for urban and agricultural working classes, 39; white men, 20–21, 119–22; women, 2, 21–22, 63–65, 106–9, 181

sugar exports, 70

Swiney, Frances, 159–60

Sydney, Australia, 88

Tanganyika, 162

Taylor, Helen, 109–10

Tel-el-Kebir, battle of, 133

Tod, Isabella, 106

Togoland, 133*f*

Transvaal, 27, 91, 128, 131

Trevelyan, Charles, 32, 76

Trevelyan, George, 85, 87

Tudors, 25

Tunisia, 132*f*

Tyndall, John, 112

Uganda, 162

uitlanders (aliens), 163

Union of South Africa, 174

United States, 27, 131, 132*f*, 133*f*, 164

universal manhood suffrage, 20

University of London, 105

upper classes; aristocracy, 13–14, 24, 57–58, 62; change in gender models, 6–7; power of, in constitutional monarchy, 39–40; separate sphere ideology, 6–7, 12–15, 29–30

urbanization, 39, 164–67

venereal disease, 144–50, 158–59

Victor, Christian, Prince (grandson), 171

Victoria, Queen, *16*, 37, *38*, *45*, *55*, *95*, *97*, *127*, *130*, *163*, *173*; birth, 1–2; childhood years, *16*, 19–20; death, *173*, 174; education, 17–19; fitness to rule, 38; goddaughter, 73, *73*–74; marriage years, *45*, 45–48, 51; pregnancy impacting, 52–56, 61;

mourning; for Brown, 100–101; for Prince Albert, 93–96, *95*; pregnancy, 52–56, *55*, 61; wedding, early married life, *45*, 45–47, 51–52; widowhood, 93–96, *95*

Victoria of Saxe-Coburg, Duchess of Kent (mother), 3, 17–19

Victoria "Vicky" Adelaide Mary Louisa, Princess Royal (daughter), 53

Voortrekkers, 90

Wakefield, Edward Gibbon, 88

Wales, 23*f*, 24

wearing apparel, gender concepts impacting, 6

Webb, William, 69

welfare programs, 177–79

Wellington, Duke of, 36

West Indies, 26–27, 70–71

Whigs, 8, 14, 20, 38

Wilberforce, William, 11, 24, 33

Wilhelm, Kaiser, 164

William IV, King, 14, 36

Windsor castle, 61–62

Winnipeg, 119

Wolseley, Garnet Joseph, 119, 128, 133–34, 171, 187

womanhood; Britons as heroic defenders of, 34; Cobbett, A., on, 13; dual concept of, 144–50; evangelical ideal of, 4–6, 14, 24; is *solidaire*, 148; primacy of female sexual function, 159; queen as mother figure, 105, *130*, 167

women. *See also* gender roles; identified exclusively by sexual function, 42; as measure of civilization, 15, 30–32, 33, 86; myths about foreign, 26; in politics, 2, 63; Queen Caroline affair impacting, 9–15; race degeneration blamed on mothers, 176–77; suppression of, 26–27

women rights/suffrage, 105; coverture versus, 152–53; critique of great Nature argument, 110–11; critique of marital relations, 154–60; ideas of British masculinity versus, 144–50; letters to Gladstone about, 185–86; New Woman authors, 153–55; suffrage, 2, 21–22, 63–65, 106–9; voting rights equal to men, 181

Women's Social and Political Union, 180

working classes; average earnings of, 7; campaign to enfranchise men, 119–22; economic hardship of, 7–8, 38–39; enfranchisement of urban and agricultural, 39; identify with Queen Caroline plight, 13; middle class women as instructors/ models for, 5–6; political alliance with radicals, 8, 14,

20, 38; Queen Caroline celebrated by, 13; race degeneration blamed on mothers of,
176–77; separate sphere
ideology among, 12–13,
38–39
World War I, 180

Yoruba people, 73, 73–74

Zanzibar, 133*f*, 162
Zimbabwe, 162
Zulu people, 89–91, 128–30,
130, 188